D0965486

What Matters

What Matters

Words of Wisdom, Hope,
and Love

J. Philip Wogaman

Abingdon Press
Nashville

WHAT MATTERS
WORDS OF WISDOM, HOPE, AND LOVE

Library of Congress Cataloging-in-Publication Data has been requested.

ISBN 978-1-5018-5979-3

18 19 20 21 22 23 24 25 26—10 9 8 7 6 5 4 3 2 1
MANUFACTURED IN THE UNITED STATES OF AMERICA

To our grandchildren
Carolyn Martha
Pinkney Susannah
John Philip II
Carrie Adelaide
Paul Joseph Jr.
Emily Margaret
Ella Jill
Deborah Anneliese

and others of their millennial generation

CONTENTS

INTRODUCTION

During the height of the Cold War, the Czech people sought to combine economic socialism with political democracy. Their "Prague Spring" was ruthlessly suppressed by an invasion by other Soviet Bloc countries. Soon after, on a fact-finding visit to Czechoslovakia, I spoke with a disillusioned graduate student. He had been a Marxist but was embittered by the collapse of the hoped-for "socialism with a human face." He was familiar with American turmoil over civil rights and the Vietnam War. After a searching conversation, he turned to me with a plaintive question, "What is there to believe?" I did not offer him easy answers, any of which he'd have rejected out of hand. But his question has continued to haunt me over the past half century. I think he voiced a question that generations of young people have felt through these years. By asking "What is there to believe?" the young

Czech student was posing the main point of this book: what matters?

In her 1934 book *Patterns of Culture*, anthropologist Ruth Benedict interviewed an elderly California Native American chief. She asked him about the huge cultural changes his people faced with the arrival and dominance of Euro-American people. As described by Benedict, the chief leaned his head back and spoke: "In the beginning God gave to every people a cup, a cup of clay, and from this cup they drank their life. They all dipped in the water, but their cups were different. Our cup is broken now. It has passed away."

With that striking metaphor, the old man spoke of the deep sense of cultural homelessness his people faced. It was all gone. What was there to live for now?

When I study the younger generation, what I see too often is this same cultural hopelessness. The world is cruel and unjust and—in the Native American chief's words— broken. Human culture is like the water fish swim in and the air we mammals breathe. Fish, I'm sure, are not particularly aware of water. It is simply where they are and where they always have been. Culture is something like that for us. It is made up of inherited language, symbols, traditions, values, myths, and shared perceptions of reality. We mostly take it for granted, at least until it is threatened.

Young people today appear to be very much at home in this culture: the music, the online interactions, clothing trends, new technologies. But what I've found beneath the surface of this dynamic activity is a deep sense of meaninglessness, that there is no great purpose to our existence. Without purpose to one's life, there is significant sorrow.

This book is prompted by two things: my great love for my grandchildren and their generation, and my concern about the world they are inheriting from those of us in older generations. It is primarily written for young people. They are beginning to raise serious questions about who they are. They are concerned about the society in which they will become active participants. They care about the world they will help forge. Above all, in serious moments, they wonder about the ultimate meaning of life. I also hope readers no longer so young will be prompted to share their own thoughts with their children, grandchildren, and other young people. And I hope this book will help foster intergenerational conversation about the things that matter.

This is a very difficult time to grow up. In some respects, it is much more challenging than when I was young. I was born in 1932. The world had just gone into what later was called the Great Depression. I have vivid childhood memories of the economic deprivations of families like ours who were unable to afford a refrigerator or an automobile. Our own family did not suffer unduly, compared with many others. I was too young for military service during World War II, but I was old enough to have clear recollections of what our country experienced on the home front.

During the late 1940s, I faced uncertainty about my vocation. That wasn't easy. But the situation people of my generation faced in childhood and youth was much simpler than what young people face today. We could choose our life's work with reasonable assurance that, with a strong work ethic, we'd be able to find opportunities and lifelong fulfillment. Many boys grew up to follow their fathers into a factory or farm, expecting to spend their whole working lives with the same company or family farm. Girls anticipated being home-makers and mothers. If they wanted to work, their options were teaching, nursing, or secretarial work. Others of us could choose a career path such as law, medicine, teaching, or in my case, ministry. We expected that after our years of preparation, we would enjoy a lifetime career. (That didn't work out for everyone, of course, but it did for the majority of us.)

Today it's a different story. Today, the challenges facing the younger generation are partly economic, with clouded employment prospects and fewer clear career paths. Young people now anticipate a career with frequent job changes as well as the possibility of completely changing industries. There are also national and global crises to face as well as cultural challenges like searching for the answers to the deep questions of life: What is the meaning of our lives? What deeper purposes can motivate us? Does anything matter much anymore?

Those from whom I learned in my youth—my parents, grandparents, and many of my mentors—are long since deceased. I value their wisdom and insight more than I can say, as I have lived long enough to understand (and forgive) their faults and limitations. My own generation is also disappearing: high school and college classmates, colleagues, and friends. In due course we, too, will all be gone. What kind of legacies will we leave?

I have sought in this brief book to contribute some insight into attaining a life well lived for the next generation, as so many did for me. It's difficult at times for two different generations to talk with each other. I, too, was mystified when my parents offered intimate recollections of the horse-and-buggy days of their childhood—a time before cars were standard transportation and when a radio was a luxury. But maybe I can still offer words of encouragement and wisdom for any young person facing the challenges ahead.

Introduction

Like everyone else, I bring some baggage to this conversation. Some of it is my personal story, some my deep family relationships with my grandchildren. Some is intellectual, growing out of my lifetime of study of social ethics. And some of it is religious, including my church roots and increased study of religions other than my own. Most of all, I bring to the conversation a deep love for the younger generation.

In the chapters that follow, we will explore what is actually meaningful in life: what matters and what doesn't. We will look at truth, character, religion, politics, community, family, vocation, wealth, power, and fame. These pages are not an exercise in nostalgia; they are not offered as a retreat into a previous golden age. They are instead an exploration of the wisdom learned in previous generations, about the mistakes and illusions of the past as well as its enduring values and accomplishments. My hope is that you will find some truth in these pages that will help you as you grow into the leaders, teachers, and healers of the world.

CHAPTER 1

TRUTH MATTERS

In the Christian New Testament, Pontius Pilate (who sentenced Jesus to death) is reported to have asked, "What is truth?" That's a very good question! We all have an intuitive sense of what the word means, but in the broadest sense, it means ideas that represent reality. It is our perception of what is real. For example, we see the sun rise in the morning, so it is a true statement that it is a new day. Or, it is true that water freezes at thirty-two degrees Fahrenheit, for that is an observed reality. So does truth matter? Yes. Truth matters if reality matters. It matters whether we embrace and seek to understand the real world, ourselves, and our place in that world. Otherwise, we only live on illusions and believe that nothing much matters at all.

The idea of truth brings up many questions. Do our ideas have some relationship to what is real? If we are not devoted to truth, can we, ourselves, be real, living in reality? If not, isn't our life a fabric of illusions, falsehoods, and lies?

Of course, being devoted to truth doesn't necessarily mean that our perceptions of reality are always truthful or accurate. Reality is always bigger than any of us. We can know reality only in part. Great minds have struggled with the question of how we know what we know. But here's a key principle: even if we do not understand all things about truth, we don't have to be completely skeptical either. We may not know everything, but we can embrace that truth exists, that truth matters, and that it is a worthwhile endeavor to intentionally seek to grow in our understanding of truth. Let's look at several dimensions of that.

Being Truthful About Ourselves

First, we need to understand a basic truth about ourselves. The truth is you have more capabilities and potentialities than you can dream of. Let that sink in. You are more capable than you can dream of. You can be and do and achieve far more than what you think you can right now. The great tragedy is when young men and women don't believe they have important possibilities.

Let me illustrate. While my family was living near

Cambridge, England, some years ago, our son Stephen brought a high school student home for dinner one night. In the course of table conversation, I asked Steve's friend whether he planned to attend nearby Cambridge University after finishing high school. No, he replied. He had taken a test as an eleven-year-old. As a result, he had been told that he lacked the ability to become a university student. Instead, he should aim at a trade school of some sort. I hit the ceiling!

According to my son, this young man was *the* outstanding student in his chemistry class, obviously capable of pursuing studies at a postsecondary level. I pushed my son's friend to forget what he had been told years earlier. There's nothing wrong with pursuing other kinds of education or aiming at one of the trades that do not require university education, but put-downs about capabilities and possibilities should not inform anyone's beliefs about what is possible. This is true for you as well: you don't know yet all that you are capable of. Accept and rest in the truth that you are far more capable than you know today. I have no idea what happened to this young student. I hope he put the earlier wrong assessments of his capabilities aside and looked at his future with fresh eyes.

I am reminded that the greatest teachers—the ones we should listen to—are the ones who see our possibilities and encourage us. Those mentors have spotted the most important truths about us. I gratefully remember one of my graduate school mentors who told me I could do anything I set my mind to. It was a wonderfully encouraging word that gave energy to my pursuits.

Of course, it was also an overstatement. It certainly didn't mean I could do *everything*. Our early years are a time for sorting out what we want to do with our life. (No one can do it all!) What you will find is that each step of your journey in these early years prepares you for the later years. Believe in yourself now and be patient as you walk out each chapter. No experience is wasted in helping you become all that you are meant to be.

The Untruth That Whole Groups of People Are Inferior

A second truth is that all people possess the same innate value. Tragically, however, racism is alive and well in our world. We've seen it in the past with African Americans and Native Americans. In both cases, the stereotypes served the specific economic ends of Euro-Americans—in one case slavery; in the other, the seizure of land. We've seen it with the stereotype of Jews as morally, if not intellectually, deficient for two thousand years. We see it with stereotypes of women, reinforcing their secondary role in society and, in family settings, their duty to serve the self-interest of men. It has taken a very long time for our culture to begin to realize that *none of these stereotypes are true.*

Oftentimes, being treated as inferior results in loss of opportunity for people to develop their capacities and helps produce "evidence" of inferiority. Isn't it interesting that when people who are stereotyped are given real opportunities, they blossom! Look at the outstanding African American leaders whose qualities could not have been anticipated by most people during the long centuries of oppressive slavery. I have known gay and lesbian individuals who internalized social stigmas despite their true sexual orientation, finding it very difficult to "come out" even to close friends and family. The social stigmas blind many people to their moral qualities as human beings and deny them the opportunity to embrace their full humanity. But it appears that society is beginning to absorb the deeper truth about sexual identity.

It is important to note in this discussion that, despite the wonderful gifts we all have, we must also acknowledge that we all possess a "dark side." There is a bit of the good and bad, the Dr. Jekyll and Mr. Hyde, in all of us. The truth, though, is that we can surmount the worst in us and grow toward the best. We do not become perfect overnight, if ever. But we can become better day by day. In the meantime, we must not define other people as worse than ourselves, comparing the best about ourselves with the worst about the groups our culture has stereotyped.

The Truth About Our Society

Young people sometimes turn to despair as they look at society. But the third truth we must learn is that our society isn't all good and it isn't all bad. History is especially helpful in revealing this truth. It does no service to our history to ignore the worst parts or overlook the best. For instance, the civil rights movement did immense good in overcoming legacies of slavery and segregation, but it is also true that those same legacies continue to haunt us.

Do we truly understand how evil slavery was—the forcible abduction of Africans from their homes, their transport across the sea—often kept in the holds of old sailing vessels for weeks (many dying along the way)? There was the buying and selling of human beings, the brutal whippings, the forcible separation of families, the denial of opportunities to learn to read and write—enforced brutally. After the Civil War, there was the cynical ending of Reconstruction opportunities for newly freed slaves. Not a pretty picture, but a true one. The miracle, in truth, is that despite the profound inhumanities, aspects of African American culture still blossomed. Think especially of the music and the rich spiritual life that, over time, came to be recognized as important contributions to the American culture.

Truthful examination of American history affords a more rounded picture of formative leaders. Dominant, creative leaders like George Washington, Thomas Jefferson, and Alexander Hamilton are rightly celebrated for the creation of a new nation and the farsighted provisions of the US Constitution. But these celebrated leaders were also slaveholders, committed to their own economic status. Their ideals should have led to the emancipation of slaves and the formation of a society that could rid itself of that vile institution. It is noteworthy that the United States lagged behind other countries in that respect. And it is also true that, for all the democratic provisions of the Constitution and law, it took more than a hundred years for women to receive the right to vote.

Equally important, it is also true that there have been strong figures throughout American history who challenged slavery and sought full equality for women. John Quincy Adams, although not the most distinguished US president, was still a remarkable champion of abolition from his postpresidential perch in the US House of Representatives. He and many others through history remind us that, for all its flaws, the American social order has been hospitable to movements of reform. I do not wish to overstate the point, for the trajectory of change has had its ups and downs. My only plea is that we view this history with a determination to see the fullness of truth, both in its positive and negative aspects.

We will explore more about politics in a later chapter, but one word of caution: we should avoid easy labels. In politics, candidates and the parties that support them tend to define opponents by their worst flaws. Why? Because it works! It appears that many people are more motivated to vote against a candidate they dislike than to vote for one whose values and proposals they support. Such negative definitions avoid larger truths and ambiguities, however, and make it more difficult to address our disagreements in a civil way.

The Truth About Religious Traditions

Fourth, as we discuss how truth matters, we must address any untruths we find in religious traditions. (We will address religion more fully in a subsequent chapter.) Is it somehow impious (or irreligious) to question aspects of, say, the Bible that cannot be factually true? For example, is it factually conceivable that Joshua made the sun stand still long enough for his forces, under God, to defeat the Amorites? Could Noah, partly assisted by his immediate family, have constructed a boat (the ark) large enough to accommodate two of every kind of living animal on earth? For that matter, could a flood have covered the entire earth? Could Jesus have literally turned water into wine at a wedding feast or multiplied a handful of bread and fish to feed thousands of his followers? Was a star actually close enough and did it move so as to guide the Magi to Bethlehem? These illustrations only scratch the surface.

Similar problems are found in other religious traditions. For example, was the entire Qur'an actually dictated to Muhammad? Did various avatars of the God Brahman actually appear in different settings as gods in the Hindu tradition? Can Hindu and Buddhist views of reincarnation be taken literally? I mean no disrespect for religious traditions to raise such questions. If truth matters and we are committed to truth, we must ask these questions honestly.

A further question: Can we face truths contained in religious traditions other than our own? Can a Christian find truth in Buddhism? Can a Jew find truth in Islam? Can a

Muslim find truth in Hinduism? I find it unthinkable that any religious tradition, followed by millions of adherents, could be *totally* devoid of *all* truth. We need not abandon our own religious convictions to explore the truths of other religions. In fact, in our world torn by division, it is imperative there are people willing to do so.

Should We *Always* Tell the Truth?

A fifth dimension of truth is whether we should always speak it. The question of always telling the truth is prominent in many writings on ethics. If we are committed to truth, doesn't that mean we should always be truthful as we interact with others? A couple of centuries ago, the German philosopher Immanuel Kant posed the question in an essay titled "On a Supposed Right to Lie from Benevolent Motives." For Kant, truth-telling is always required for the sake of our own moral dignity and our respect for the moral dignity of others. He believed that lying is corrupting. His point is that when we lie we create distrust in relationships. If people are known to lie, how can they be trusted? Do we not appreciate those who always tell us the truth? The case for habitual truth-telling is compelling. To be a truth-teller is to be a person of integrity.

That said, are there ever exceptions? Suppose, during

the era of American slavery, you are helping to maintain the Underground Railroad, a system that facilitates the journey of slaves to freedom. You maintain one of the "stations" in the Underground Railroad—a basement in which you house a fugitive slave. Slave hunters knock at your door, looking for the runaway slave. Do you tell the truth? If so, the fugitive will be captured, probably beaten within an inch of his life, and returned to slavery. On the other hand, if you lie convincingly, the hunters may go on to the next house and your fugitive will be saved. Is absolute truth-telling in such a situation preferable to the life and future of this human being? A similar illustration could be offered for those harboring Jews whom the Gestapo were seeking during the Holocaust.

Are there other exceptions? Years ago, medical doctors often withheld a negative prognosis from a dying patient, not wishing the patient to be discouraged and give up. They believed in the end it wouldn't matter much, and for the time remaining, it might provide a bit of respite from fear. I believe most doctors no longer follow this approach, thinking it is better for a patient to plan his or her remaining time more intentionally and positively. I have always thought that to be better. In a number of pastoral experiences, I've found that dying patients usually responded courageously and positively to the bad news.

Another exception could be not sharing your opinion honestly. You might consider someone to be bad looking. Do you share that view with him or her? Somebody seems depressed; do you share that perception? In such cases we might probe deeper, sharing more positive perceptions. Let's acknowledge that sometimes a truth can hurt others. Where possible, we should find ways to reinforce that person's self-esteem—for that is the larger truth.

If we believe truth matters, we will *almost* always tell the truth. We don't need to say everything we believe all of the time, but neither should we lie. Every exception to truth-telling should have to bear the burden of proof. Some rare exceptions can meet that burden, but most of the time we should speak truth.

Is There Truth Beyond the Factual Level?

Another dimension to explore is whether truth is limited to facts. In speaking of truth as the relationship between ideas and realities, we often refer to our views of the factual world. Do our ideas conform to real facts? The world is round, not flat; that is true. A bank robber was caught on camera; his factual guilt is true. Many biologists can cite factual evidence that human beings have evolved from earlier life forms, so evolution can be considered a generally truthful account of human origins.

We are immersed in a world of facts, and our conceptions of truth are usually based upon what can be observed or demonstrated. This is why science has emerged as such an important avenue into truth. Many scientists are convinced we shouldn't treat anything as true unless it can be verified through scientific methods. While science is very helpful indeed, it is not the same thing as philosophy. It cannot provide a truthful view of all that is. Am I right in saying that science cannot provide a truthful view of all that is?

One form of philosophy, called logical positivism, would dispute such a statement. The best-known representative of logical positivism was A. J. Ayer (1910–1989). Ayer was a self-avowed atheist but with a unique twist. He didn't just regard beliefs about God and moral goodness as untruthful. He considered them to be *meaningless*. Why? Because to him the only things that are either true or false are statements subject to verification. God cannot be verified, nor for that matter can views of morality. These are subjective. We can talk about subjective, psychological facts, but these belong in the psychology department, where our subjective feelings and attitudes are examined factually.

Ayer does provide a loophole—perhaps one that is

larger than he might have supposed. He acknowledges that an idea or claim can be verifiable in principle even if we don't currently have the means of verification. For example, prior to the first moon landing in 1969, no one had ever observed the far side of the moon. Its existence and description were verifiable in principle—and therefore meaningful—even if it couldn't yet be observed. I wonder whether belief about God could fall into that category. You'd have to be godlike in some fashion to verify God factually. That is meaningful even if not practical. I'll return to that later.

Are there other forms of truth in nonfactual form that science cannot verify? Take the role of myth, for instance. A myth is typically presented as a statement about fact—what happened, when it happened, and so on. The objective framework of the myth may be totally, demonstrably nonfactual. Yet the myth can point beyond itself to deeper-level realities. Think of the American myth about George Washington chopping down the cherry tree and, when accosted by an angry parent, confessing his deed, saying, "I cannot tell a lie." The likelihood of that actually having happened is remote, but the story conveys what may be a largely truthful portrait of Washington's character. Somewhat similarly, great novels like Victor Hugo's *Les Misérables* are couched in factual terms. The story makes no claim to be an actual account of history (though Hugo's novel does have some historical material in it), but it inspires in us a larger conception of the human moral reality. These stories help us understand, ever more powerfully, why truth matters.

One of the most important aspects of philosophy is pursuit of the question, How do we know what we know? A. J. Ayer attempted to provide an answer to that, although his view, in my judgment, is incomplete. Boston philosopher Edgar S. Brightman (1884–1953) spoke about truth as "comprehensive coherence." By this he meant that conceptions of truth represent the sum total of realities of which we are aware. We take all of the information available through science and other sources, and add it together into a coherent whole. Such a view of truth may be helpful to many people.

Without disputing that, I suggest another wrinkle: which of our experiences do we find most helpful in interpreting the meaning of the whole of our experience? When we meet someone for the first time, we may be struck by some feature that defines that person, such as facial expression, tone of voice, clothing, or something else. As we learn more about the person, our views might change. Isn't that true of most of our initial perceptions of people or things about which we know very little? That is especially true about our views of all of reality, from the vast universe to the microorganisms.

Our conceptions of the whole of reality are necessarily very limited. Of course, we cannot claim to know the whole of reality. But which of our experiences seem to us to provide the best clues as to the meaning of the whole? Obviously, an A. J. Ayer finds scientifically verifiable facts to be that all-explaining clue. Others may be more persuaded by loving human relationships. Can love somehow be our best clue as to the nature and purposes of the whole? Is that, or something else, what makes the most sense about our lives?

As we think about living a meaningful life, remember that truth matters. There are things that are fundamentally true. Our conceptions of those truths are important, and our commitment to truth must be decisive if we are to realize our full potential as humans.

A Note to Younger Readers

Let your commitment to truth guide you in the years ahead. Nobody possesses all of the truth, but we have touched upon important parts of it: truth about yourself and your possibilities, truth about both the good and not-so-good aspects of our history, truth about other people and social evils, scientific insights and our own responsibility to tell the truth—at least when it will not harm others.

CHAPTER 2

CHARACTER MATTERS

No one is perfect. Even those identified as saints in various religions had imperfections—Mother Teresa, Saint Peter, Buddha, Gandhi, and Muhammad. Even Jesus is quoted by the earliest gospel as saying, "Why do you call me good? No one is good but God alone" (Mark 10:18).

That said, it matters what *kind* of person we are. There are significant differences between degrees of personal goodness. We perceive and evaluate other people by dominant moral characteristics—whether they are honest or dishonest, arrogant or humble, gregarious or reclusive, or broadly good or bad. Some characteristics are simply differences of temperament—a highly creative person may not be as extroverted, and a political leader had better not be too introverted. But the kind of character that really matters is the moral kind. Most of us can think of people we've known with real integrity. The kind of people who really care about the truth, as we discussed it in the previous chapter. We know they can be trusted and we often relax when we're around them. In contrast, we're more guarded with people who are dishonest.

In our business relationships, we really value the honesty of people with whom we're dealing. Most of us can recall having been cheated or lied to, and conversely, we remember those who were in a position to take advantage of us but didn't.

Once, when our children were much younger, we were driving across the very hot Mojave Desert at night, heading toward Las Vegas. The car began to sputter. Something was wrong. We continued slowly to Las Vegas, arriving there in the morning. We found a service garage. I feared the worst. Were we looking at a major repair? After examining the engine, the mechanic smiled and said the only thing wrong was a defective spark plug, replaceable for a few dollars. Reflecting on the incident, it occurred to me the mechanic could have said anything and gotten away with it, including a major repair. But he was obviously an honest man. That certainly mattered to us financially!

Think about the number of services we depend on where the person diagnosing the problem is also the one who will fix it. Isn't that a built-in conflict of interest? By diagnosing this as a more serious problem, the server can prescribe a more expensive solution from which he or she will benefit financially. Fortunately, many (I believe most) service providers have higher professional standards based on their character. We have to depend upon the serviceperson's integrity, and soon enough we identify who we can trust and who we can't.

Honesty is a huge part of our character. It helps define who we are. We forget that our own credibility is at risk when we frequently tell untruths. The problem with lying is that it not only shows disrespect for others but it affects their ability to trust us. Communication can deteriorate quickly if honesty and trust are broken.

Can We Actually Change Our Basic Character?

The first question we may ask ourselves is whether we can change our character. Are we genetically, biologically programmed to be what we are in character as well as what we are physically? Don't we all know infants and small children who seem to be good by their very nature while others seem more difficult? Part of that may be attributed to differences in parenting or unrealized needs, but differences can appear even in the same family.

In recent years there have been great advances in scientific studies of the brain. They show we may be much more programmed than we thought. Even apart from recent studies, we've long known that, through hypnosis, people can be led to act in ways having little to do with their conscious intentions. I'm certainly no expert on the sciences lying behind studies of the brain, but I do not lightly dismiss the broad implications of such studies. If we are indeed predetermined, the view that "character matters" may still be true, but then there isn't much we can do about it.

However, I'm not ready to accept the conclusion that there is little we can do to change our character. My counsel to young people is to remain skeptical about any view that says we are not responsible for our character or behavior—even if a lot of who we are is prefigured biologically and situationally.

How can we improve our character? Perhaps we can take a cue from the medieval Catholic philosopher and theologian Thomas Aquinas. Following the ancient Greek philosopher Aristotle, Aquinas spoke of virtue as a "habit of the will toward a good end." By contrast, a vice is a habit of the will taking us away from the good.

We all know what habits are. We develop them and rely on them all of the time. Life would be incredibly difficult if everything we did had to be thought through. Early in life, I learned to tie my shoelaces, brush my teeth, walk, and run. Later, I learned to throw a ball, tie a necktie, and shave. These and countless other things came to be second nature. I didn't have to think much about them. To be sure—and this is important—none of these habits came automatically. They had to be learned and practiced. Similarly no great musician was born with the skills needed to play an instrument. A violinist has to work hard for years. At first, the music squeaks; later, it can become deeply moving. Constant practice is necessary. After many years, the violinist's hand movements become habitual so she can concentrate on the music itself. Isn't that process of habit formation characteristic of much, even most, of our living?

I believe it is also true of our acquisition of virtuous habits—being good, habitually. Following Aquinas's definition, our character is the sum of the virtues or vices that have become second nature to us. If so, then we can definitely improve our character. We can work at becoming better people.

The apostle Paul wrote what some have described as his love poem. It is about how we can become more loving. While the thirteenth chapter of 1 Corinthians is part of the Christian New Testament, it could readily be embraced by morally serious people who identify with other religions. To Paul, the overall defining element of good character is love. But *love* can mean many different things to different people in different cultures. Without further explanation, the word can become a platitude or an empty abstraction. Notice how Paul gives the idea of love more specific content. You could almost say that Paul is speaking about the disciplines of love:

> If I speak in the tongues of mortals and of angels, but do not have love, I am a noisy gong or a clanging cymbal. And if I have prophetic powers, and understand all mysteries and all knowledge...but do not have love, I am nothing....
>
> Love is patient; love is kind; love is not envious or boastful or arrogant or rude. It does not insist on its own way; it is not irritable or resentful; it does not rejoice in wrongdoing, but rejoices in the truth. It bears all things, believes all things, hopes all things, endures all things.
>
> Love never ends....When I was a child, I spoke like a child, I thought like a child, I reasoned like a child; when I became an adult, I put an end to childish ways. (1 Corinthians 13:1-2, 4-8, 11)

Taken as a whole, this is quite a portrait of good character.

What Love Is *Not*

You will notice this passage on love includes both the positive and negative—positively, it gives the attitudes and behaviors to be cultivated; negatively, it states what is to be resisted. I'd like to start with the negatives—what love is *not*.

Love is not envious. Envy creates a barrier between people. We envy the possessions or power or status of others. We want what they have. How do we resist envy? Sometimes it isn't easy. Later, when we're a bit older, we may see the emptiness of some of the things we've envied. In the meantime, the best advice I can give is to study the personhood of those whose things we envy. That can partly be a matter of cultivating friendships if that person is accessible, or it can mean deeper study of those we can't know personally. We're likely to discover that those who have attracted our envy are troubled people. This is often the case with those who have extreme wealth or fame. Then we can pause to take stock of the gifts we already have. In the words of an old hymn, "Count your many blessings, name them one by one." Such responses to the beginnings of envy are disciplines of love and they are liberating.

Love is not boastful. Boastfulness is usually an unsuccessful effort to elevate ourselves at the expense of others.

"Look at what we've done!" Other people tend to resent our boastfulness. It actually creates another barrier. When tempted to boast of our accomplishments or possessions, we can develop the discipline of complimenting others on *their* gifts. If you're a candidate for a job or political office, you have to find ways to draw attention to your qualifications. But keep in mind that people are more attracted to restraint.

Some years ago, a couple was visiting Denmark. While in Copenhagen, they ran into a friendly man in one of the parks. He was helpful in directing them and explaining some things about Denmark. He asked where they were from and what they did. After quite some time of talking about themselves, they asked him what he did. "Oh," he remarked, "I'm the king of this country." Sure enough, he was the king of Denmark! There was his face staring at them on the currency! Imagine the lost opportunity of learning more about this man because you were too occupied with your own self. We don't have to reject our own gifts and accomplishments, but we can discipline ourselves to avoid boasting. Obviously the Danish king felt no need to boast.

Love is not arrogant. This should be pretty obvious. When we exaggerate our own importance in comparison with others, we create more barriers. We all should embrace the truth that our lives are important, but arrogance is treating the lives of other people as unimportant. When tempted to speak or act in an arrogant manner, we should stifle the temptation. After repeating this for a time, we won't be inclined to act arrogantly. Similarly, Paul writes that rudeness is contrary to love. That is not just a counsel of politeness; it is regard for the feelings of others. One point I have to keep reminding myself of is not to interrupt when others are speaking—not even when I'm sure the person speaking is mistaken. There can be gentler ways of drawing forth a truth to be shared.

Love does not insist on its own way. This is a willingness to compromise (not on the important things, of course). It is an acknowledgment that our way may not be the only way or even the best way. By not always insisting on our own way, we can be saved from serious mistakes, although I do not think that was what Paul had in mind. He was aware that people who impose their will on others are showing disrespect. When, in the vernacular way of speaking, we say, "My way or the highway," we're putting ourselves before others. That is hardly a way to show regard, much less love, for others.

Love is not irritable or resentful. Any of us can be irritated, often with good reason. This is the habit of looking more deeply at the source of our irritation. If our irritability or resentfulness is the result of a hostile act or attitude by another person, we can try not to take it personally. Instead,

25

we can ask ourselves *why* this has been said or done, and try to rise above it. How many families have been torn apart by resentments harbored through the years? Paul encourages us to break through the resentments and try to restore broken relationships.

These aspects of love may or may not seem obvious, but they can lead to more positive habits of mind and will. Character is the accumulation, over time, of habits that encompass positive virtues and that resist temptations that are contrary to love.

What Love *Is*

You will notice the positives about love in Paul's writing are specific. They are not empty sentiments. They are virtues to be cultivated in a disciplined way so they become habits of the will.

Love is patient. What is patience? It can be defined as taking the necessary time—no less and no more. Good parents who love their children dearly have to be patient. Children don't grow up overnight. If young people are pushed too hard too fast, it can actually slow down their development. Good parents know there are times to push, but there are also times to bite one's tongue and accept immaturities. Doesn't that apply to all loving relationships between people? Know when to push but also when to show restraint. Becoming a patient person means developing this action as a habit. In the same way, we have to be a bit more patient with ourselves! We're not going to become perfect overnight.

Are there some things about which we shouldn't be patient? Maybe so. If there are behaviors, practices, customs, or laws that should no longer be tolerated, it can indicate that the necessary time to change has arrived. One of Martin Luther King Jr.'s books was titled *Why We Can't Wait*. His point was that the time had come to get rid of racist institutions and practices. He made the same point in his famous "Letter from Birmingham Jail" in response to a misguided plea from white religious leaders that he should slow down. The fact was King was very patient where he had to be in working through the movement for change.

Love is kind. It's easy to see that—*kindness* is almost a synonym for *love*. But how do we cultivate kindness? Some people seem to be born with a kind disposition, but not many. Kindness is also something to be worked at. Many years ago I was a Boy Scout. I recall the rule that we should do a good turn daily. It might be helping an elderly person across the street or running an errand for someone. Kindness can become habitual if we are intentional about it. Perhaps we see someone hurting physically or psychologically. We may not be able to take the hurt away, but we can communicate our caring. We can reach out to people who have been rejected or stigmatized by society with a word of acceptance or an invitation to do something together. Pause now to recall acts of kindness you've received and how those acts expressed the character of the people doing them. Needless to say, cruelty is the exact opposite of kindness. Any impulse to do or say something cruel must be resisted.

Love rejoices in the truth. That doesn't refer to rejoicing in true but harmful gossip about other people! Paul has written that love doesn't rejoice in wrongdoing. How often, in a highly competitive society, we are tempted to welcome evidence that a competitor or someone we don't like has done something wrong. The political scene, even in a democracy, puts a premium on tearing down the opposition. Candidates for high office typically have research teams looking for bad things about the opposition in order to shape public opinion of that person. Doesn't something like that also happen in more intimate relationships? We may feel we can gain greater acceptance in a group if we expose the wrongdoing of those who don't belong, but love rejoices in the positive truth about others rather than focuses on their inevitable flaws.

Love bears all things…endures all things. Love doesn't give up. We may have to sacrifice and endure hardship for the sake of love. I have never been in battle, but I've often heard about combatants who risk their lives, not so much for the larger strategic objectives, but because they care about the survival of their fellow soldiers. This can be true in ordinary life as well. During my years as a pastor, I saw incredible heroism by and for loved ones. One example that stands out was a woman who was diagnosed with terminal cancer. As a cancer nurse, she knew exactly what that would mean for her. Knowing she would have to face increasing pain, she decided to keep doses of morphine to an absolute minimum—despite the pain—so she could be fully present to her family. The lesson here for all of us is to not give up on one another.

Love believes and hopes all things. Paul was not urging us to be gullible. He was urging us to believe in the good despite evidences to the contrary. We hope for the good. We can all think of teachers and mentors who believed in us even more than we could believe in ourselves. I mentioned one of my own mentors in chapter 1. I expect we can all remember those who have had such an impact on our lives. Believing and hoping all things is a reminder to be intentional about looking for the possibilities in other people.

Paul's words show us that character can be acquired, bit by bit, as we venture through life. We have to work at it, but moral character is its own reward. It truly matters both in the fulfillment of our own lives and in the wider social context of which we are a part.

The Virtue of Humility

The danger in emphasizing what we can do to develop character is that we might then become proud of that achievement—like the old quip about "humility and how I attained it." The whole point of character is to grow beyond self-centeredness. Growing in character is to acknowledge our continuing need to *grow*. We never fully arrive. As Paul's great passage illustrates, as we grow in love, we become more conscious of the goodness in others. When we are tempted toward excessive pride, it is a good exercise to think more consciously of the gifts and accomplishments of others. This is not a false humility. It doesn't mean denying our own importance. It is to see ourselves in true perspective. I am struck by how often in the biographies of saints one reads that their biggest struggle is often at exactly this point. The modern-day Saint Teresa is an example. She saw herself in perspective, knowing her weaknesses and the strengths of others, but this didn't happen overnight. It was a lifelong effort to grow spiritually.

Humility means looking for the good in others, but strangely, humility is also relating more kindly to those who don't seem to be good. One of the hallmarks of humility is to be compassionate toward people who are not of good character—or don't appear to be. Humility is also understanding we never quite know the reasons for the moral failings of other people. Because of this there is no room for moral superiority.

Honesty, love, and humility are tremendously important to living life well. Who we are, how we act, and the habits we build impact ourselves and our world immeasurably.

A Note to Younger Readers

Remember these words from Shakespeare's Hamlet: "This above all: to thine own self be true. And it must follow, as the night the day, Thou canst not then be false to any man." Shakespeare is talking about character. We have seen the importance of integrity, not simply as treating others honestly, but as growing in our capacity to love. With diligence, the virtues that make up character can be acquired bit by bit, until they become habitual.

CHAPTER 3

RELIGION MATTERS

It may take some doing to convince some in the younger generation that religion matters. Recent studies, especially those of the Pew Research Center, have clearly demonstrated a falling away from religious commitments by increasing numbers of young people. More than a third of the next generation have been described as "nones." The term comes from those who check "none" in questionnaires of religious preferences. Interestingly, a majority of the millennials who have no religious affiliation were raised in families that were involved in religion. Historically, a very large majority of Americans have identified as Protestant or Catholic, but in seven short years (2007–2014) the Christian share of the population fell from 78.4 percent to 70.6 percent. So the decline among millennials is but the most visible part of a wider trend. There has been a discernible decline in the number of people of all ages with religious affiliation. That needs to be taken seriously, and not just defensively, by those who remain religiously committed. One must look at the reasons why many have abandoned religious traditions and commitments. Even those who remain committed can learn something.

Why Have So Many Young People Given Up on Religion?

The reasons for the decline are doubtless complex. Some conservative Christians, such as members of the unofficial United Methodist "Good News Movement," argue it is because the churches have abandoned the traditions of the faith, including biblical authority. Many conservatives argue that churches have become too liberal about some of the hot-button moral issues. The truth is probably exactly the opposite!

Many young people consider church teaching on some of those issues to be badly out of step with the times. One thirty-year-old, interviewed on an NPR panel, made the point: "Starting in middle school, we got the lessons about why premarital sex was not OK, why active homosexuality was not OK. Growing up in American culture, kids automatically pushed back on those things." She found she had to abandon

her Roman Catholic community because she could no longer accept "a lot of these core beliefs." She was probably
speaking for many young people who can no longer accept
conservative beliefs espoused by the religious groups they
grew up in. That may be especially true in religious settings
where open, honest discussion is discouraged. The easiest
thing can be just to walk away.

Younger people often accuse organized religion of
being hypocritical. The people they see in religious settings
just don't live up to what they profess. I'll say more about this
later, but the problem isn't simply one of failure to live out
one's faith; it can be a disinclination to do so. The problem of
hypocrisy is visibly evident when religious leaders fall short.
It can appear that such leaders enjoy the power and privi-
leges of their position and care little about moral or spiritual
integrity.

Even beyond the moral failings of religious people, the
religious traditions themselves may no longer appear truthful or even honest. As we noted in the first chapter, sacred
Scriptures can seem, and often are, clearly incompatible
with scientific evidence. Scientific conclusions are based
on serious examination of facts. What appear to be factual
reports in Scripture may represent the honest beliefs of the
writers, but their ways of getting at the facts are, by modern

standards, primitive. In some instances, the stories may have been written to make larger points, not to be taken factually. Those who want to take all factual claims in Scripture literally try to rationalize them in one way or another. However, we shouldn't be surprised that many young people, who have been exposed to rigorous science, remain skeptical. True, many Christians find no contradiction between science and the deeper meaning of Scriptures, finding them mutually enriching; others reject scientific findings that are in conflict with a literal reading of the Bible. For example, well-established scientific evidence for human evolution is in conflict with a literal reading of creation stories in Genesis, and scientific understandings of the cosmos mean that the sun could not have stood still to give Joshua longer to defeat an enemy, nor could a single star have moved ahead of the Magi in their search for the newborn Jesus.

The problem is not limited to Christians or Jews, of course. Many Muslims believe the Qur'an was literally dictated to the prophet Muhammad. Non-Muslims have a hard time with that. Buddhism is less committed to literal details about how Siddhārtha Gautama came to enlightenment as the Buddha, but the story is still important to Buddhism.

Even more than the intellectual problems one can have with the factual accuracy of many religious traditions is

35

the problem with what can be called the dark side, that is, aspects of the traditions that can no longer be accepted for moral reasons. What are we to say, for instance, about a conception of God who would drown virtually all of humanity because of human sinfulness? Or the killing of every man, woman, and child in Jericho? Or the culmination of history in the great battle of Armageddon in which the enemies of God will be ruthlessly slaughtered? And what about the commandments in Leviticus calling for people to be stoned to death for what would today be considered, at worst, only minor sins? There are similar problems in some of the other great religions as well.

In light of all that, the nones of the younger generation can be pardoned for giving up on religion. Even those who were raised in one of its forms can be pardoned.

But Not So Fast! There May Be More to "Religion" Than That

Many younger people may not realize that generations of theologians and philosophers, even well before the twenty-first century, dealt with such issues. Critical study of Scriptures began more than two hundred years ago; and even from the early years of Christianity, there were thinkers who were aware of what I've called the "dark side" and understood that much of the received tradition should be treated metaphorically or as forms of analogy. For example, that was notably true of the great Alexandrian thinkers Clement and Origen in the third century CE.

Such points aside, we should ask "What is religion?" before writing it off. Is religion just what you see in organized, institutional form and in sacred writings? It has some connection with that, of course, but the definition must be deeper. The philosopher-theologian Paul Tillich defined religion as whatever we hold as our "ultimate concern." What is it that concerns us most? What do we care most about? Another theologian, H. Richard Niebuhr, wrote about our "center of value." He asks, "What is it that we value so much that it is the basis of our attitude toward everything else?" We all have a center of value, whether we're conscious of it or not. It comprises our views about what matters and what doesn't.

By these definitions, *everyone* is religious! Everyone has ultimate concerns. Everyone has some kind of value center. That includes the active adherents of all religions. It also includes agnostics and even atheists. Often, people are not consciously aware of this reality, but it is a reality nevertheless. The point is missed, however, if we define religion only in institutional terms or if we restrict it to belief in a particular conception of God. I even dare to say that everybody *worships*, even if only unconsciously. Sometimes what people worship is contrary to what they profess. For instance, someone might belong to a particular organized religion, even attending worship services regularly, but his or her real worship might be of materialism, power, or fame.

Then, Does What We "Worship" Matter?

If we're all worshipping something, does it matter *what* we worship? Well, yes. We live by and for our values. They define who we are and what we want to accomplish. That doesn't mean all of our values are embraced in the deep sense of worship, but all of our lesser values are to a considerable degree a reflection of our value center. They express what is ultimately important to us. The word *worship* is derived from "worth." We worship what we take to have ultimate worth.

Seen in that perspective, I want to affirm much of what I see in the attitudes and values of this younger generation. This may not be true of everybody, but most millennials seem to care deeply about others. They are often committed to justice, being more tolerant of human differences and accepting diversity as a gift and not as a problem. On the whole, young people tend to be less racist, sexist, xenophobic, and homophobic than my generation. That may suggest the presence of a deeper center of value that some may not be consciously aware of. That center of value, even if held subconsciously, is what matters most to us.

Yes, religious worship matters. But it may matter even more what *kind* of religion. My hope is that young people will find it possible to worship God as the source of all that is and come to understand that God cares for each of us. That is a matter of faith, not of factual proof. Limited human beings like us can scarcely comprehend the vastness and timelessness of God. This universe, with its hundreds of billions of galaxies, each with millions, perhaps billions of stars, is real but incomprehensibly vast. If God is the source of all that is, then God is timeless. The mind boggles. How could there ever have been a time before God (or material reality) existed? But how could there ever have been absolute nothingness? I can't solve that riddle, but I don't believe anyone else can either. In the end, it comes down to faith. Not the kind of faith that ignores facts, but faith as to the reality behind all facts. As the first chapter makes clear, ultimate reality is clouded in mystery.

My own belief has partly been a result of serious study and thought, but more than that, it has been the result of my seeking to make sense out of my own life. I was born into a Christian home—my father was even a minister. From earliest childhood, I saw myself as belonging to God. That faith, however, did not continue without struggle. My childhood conceptions of God went from a kind of oblong object in the heavens to a Father figure (as suggested by Jesus) to an all-encompassing reality. I experienced periods of doubt, coming to realize, eventually, that doubt can be a friend of faith and not its enemy. Doubt can help expose error and evil. In later years, partly through the insights of Paul Tillich, I came to see that God is not an object alongside other things—God is the source and support of all things. I'm both amused and challenged by Tillich's wry comment that God does not exist, for only things exist, and God is more than a thing. My journey of faith continues, knowing that the reality of God is far too great for me ever to understand it all. But basic to that faith is recognition that somehow God is defined by love and that the whole universe somehow has love at its heart.

Another way to get at the reality of God is by our view of revelation. For some, revelation is like a strike of lightning—God speaking out of the blue. A better way to understand revelation, in terms we explored in chapter 1, is to see that all of us take some aspects of our experience as the best clues to the nature of the mystery of reality. Reality is bigger than any of us, but what helps us most to understand it?

Different kinds of experience will be taken in this way by

different people, but I would like to think that the best or "highest" form of reality of which we are aware is human life itself. One writer, James Carroll, put it this way in saying why he continued to believe in God: "I hold the faith not because religion can prove its claims for God, but because those claims can make a cosmos that includes self-knowing creatures more intelligible, not less." So, he continued, "Proof is not the key; it is irrelevant." He doesn't claim to have proved anything, certainly not in a way that a scientifically minded person could accept. Nevertheless, religious faith helps us make sense of the universe.

But worship is more than that. Ultimately, we can't worship what we don't believe. Why would we worship anything less than what we consider to be the source of everything else? Perhaps there has to be some unity between what is true and what is good.

That is why Jesus Christ is so central to the faith of Christians. It is not because of any kind of Christian exclusivism; it is not the idea that Jesus had existed from all eternity and was "sent" to earth by God. Such views can contain a larger truth if not taken literally. It is because of the profound love of Jesus, best exemplified by his willingness to die on the cross. That was the culmination of a depth of love shown throughout his life. Christians trust that the love of Jesus is

41

from God and that it is central to the nature of God. If God is love, then God is worthy of worship.

Can We Be Spiritual Without Being Religious?

Many in the younger generation talk about being spiritual without being religious. Is this possible? Perhaps not, at least not as I have defined religion. We are all religious. We all worship, even if what we worship is far removed from what religious traditions say about God.

But there is a broader question. Can we be spiritually *individualistic* in the way we hold and express our religion? The short answer is maybe so. Haven't we all experienced spiritual renewal at moments when we were not surrounded by other people? Perhaps it was while reading an especially uplifting book, or while enjoying the beauties of nature on a long hike, or while engaging in meditative practices.

The longer answer, however, is that it may be more difficult than you think to be "spiritual" apart from some kind of social context. We are all social beings. We live in and through our relationships. I find it almost inconceivable that anyone could be *fully* spiritual all by herself or himself. Our deeper values—our center of value—is enhanced, nurtured, and supported as it is shared with others. Even if I were an atheist (which I'm not), I'd still want to have some kind of group through which I could express humanistic values. There have been recent efforts by some atheists to form organizations and a kind of worship that is consistent with their beliefs. It may be difficult to sustain even an atheistic view of things in isolation from like-minded people.

Times of shared worship can make all of us better. We are inspired by the witness of fellow believers, by great hymns, by Scriptures, by sermons that take us beyond our narrow self-centered and materialistic values into a deeper sense of our place in the whole of reality. In times of sorrow, we find comfort. In place of bitterness, we find love. In place of despair we find hope. We are strengthened by the views and values of others and of our shared traditions. All this in spite of the imperfections of all of us.

I suspect that many who speak about being spiritual without being religious are reacting against a kind of mechanical conformity to a *form* of worship. Do we have to take literally everything that is said in worship? Must we adhere to forms of worship legalistically? No. Worship forms, for their own sake, are not real worship.

Quaker meetings gather in silence, meditating, until someone breaks the silence with a spiritual insight to share with others. No hymns, no sermon, no sacraments. High Anglican worship is centered in the *Book of Common Prayer,* with union recitation of written prayers and a central place for the Eucharist, or Holy Communion. Other mainstream Protestant churches place heavy emphasis on a sermon preached by an ordained clergyperson. Roman Catholic worship centers in the Mass. Even within the same denomination, the forms of worship can vary greatly. Music, too, is a form of worship that many enjoy. But remember: a form of worship is not worship.

True worship, while not irrational, involves *deep feeling*. Since by nature we are social creatures, our deeper feelings can be enhanced—not diminished—by joining with others in worship. Even art expressed through music, poetry, or painting is social in its deeper context. Most people who enjoy art are drawn into a kind of union with the artist and with the artist's vision of what is ultimately real. And that is the point: to be spiritual means we need to worship, and corporate worship should point us past the traditions and forms of worship to something greater.

But What About the Hypocrisies of Religious Bodies?

Another reason many young people reject religion is because of hypocrisy. Hypocrisy is not to be celebrated. This is obvious. However, if hypocrisy is failing to live up to our highest values, then who of us is not, to some extent, hypocritical? None of us is immune. (If you do always live up to your highest standards, that may mean that your standards aren't high enough!)

The worst hypocrisy of all is proclaiming moral values we have no intention of keeping ourselves. Some televangelists have exploited large audiences for material gain. Some clergy have exploited parishioners, even children, sexually while preaching a legalistic sexual ethic. A whole lot of people have wanted to be seen in church (or in other religious settings) primarily for purposes of social prestige or other personal gain. I don't wonder why many young people say that church hypocrisy has turned them off of religion. I applaud their honesty.

Those of us who maintain religious commitments must keep improving. Perhaps none of us can live up to our highest values, but that must not be for lack of trying. When religious language speaks of us all as sinners, this is not to endorse sin. It is an expression of realism about the human condition, and it is framed in regret.

Another source of widespread hypocrisy is seen in corporate religious history. This is very discouraging. Keep in mind, though, that in religion, like history, the picture is always mixed. Religion has housed forces of evil and injustice; it has also inspired dedicated efforts to overcome evil and injustice. The two opposing movements are threaded together throughout religious history.

Looking at organized religion in this and other countries, we actually find a lot of good. Most religious communities are caring associations of people. This is almost universally true of small churches, synagogues, and mosques. People pray for one another in times of suffering and sorrow. Whether such prayers cause God to intervene physically is beside the point; the prayers bespeak concern and lead to actions of outreach. Someone has died, so a flood of food arrives for grieving survivors. Somebody is ill, so fellow members of the religious body arrive to offer moral support. Someone needs counsel and receives it—not just from professionals but from fellow believers. Somebody needs a ride to work and gets it. Do such acts of kindness occur everywhere, all the time? No. But these actions are the opposite of hypocrisy, and they are frequent.

The dark side of corporate religious history is tied to the good. The acts of kindness within a religious community often exclude people who are not a part of that community. Exclusive attitudes toward the outsider are also a form of hypocrisy. That is especially the case where stigmatized people have been excluded through prejudice. For many years, African Americans were systematically excluded from participation in southern white churches, and such exclusion was not limited to the South either. A number of predominantly Black denominations were formed as a direct result of African Americans being treated as inferior. In our own time, those who have been publicly identified as gay or lesbian have been ostracized in many churches.

My own Methodist denomination has also housed leading segregationists, such as John Satterfield. Satterfield was at the same time (in the 1950s) a leader in national Methodist circles and a leader in the White Citizens' Council of his native Mississippi. Governor George Wallace was a practicing Methodist (as, however, was George McGovern!). In Africa, the Dutch Reformed denomination resolutely supported apartheid (though it was successfully demolished by the Anglican archbishop Desmond Tutu and the nation's new president, Methodist Nelson Mandela).

Yet if religious bodies have often fostered discrimination, they have also been in the very forefront of movements to combat discrimination. In the American religious scene, religious bodies have typically led the struggles for social justice. Today's younger generation knows a lot about the civil rights movement, but it can be easy to forget that it was thoroughly religious in motivation and action. Led by figures like the Reverends (I emphasize the title) Martin Luther King Jr., Ralph Abernathy, and Andrew Young, church buildings were often the action centers. The pivotal struggles in Selma, Alabama, were centered at the Brown Chapel AME Church in Selma. Northern churches and synagogues were recruitment centers for people going south to join the movements. Denominational bodies provided funds and other resources to help. I saw much of that firsthand, and I can testify to its intensity and effectiveness.

The civil rights movement is not the only example of religious leadership in social justice causes. The nineteenth- and early-twentieth-century feminist movement for the equal citizenship rights of women is another example. Even the labor movement had serious religious backing despite its largely secular leadership. The Social Gospel leader Walter Rauschenbusch helped mobilized national sentiment for Progressive Era reforms and for the labor movement. During World War 2, American churches embarked on a massive crusade for a new world order that helped mobilize support for creation of the United Nations. Most of the leading denominations have adopted large numbers of resolutions in support of progressive social principles. Religious support for social justice has been widespread. In reading the writings of contemporary atheists, I am struck by how little attention is given to these realities. Honest criticism of religion cannot ignore that.

Filled with historic movements of justice as well as cruel hypocrisy, religion has mattered throughout history and matters today for future generations. The only question is how we choose to embody and express religion in our own lives. My hope is that this younger generation will move beyond cynicism and despair about religion to find religious communities where they feel at home spiritually and where they can join with others in making religion matter for good and not for ill.

A Note to Younger Readers

This is an especially critical chapter. Our fundamental values shape everything about our lives. Do you agree that everyone has a religion? Does it matter what kind? Do you agree that Christians shouldn't make exclusive claims, even though we believe that Jesus Christ helps us see that the nature of God is love? Do we need to connect with other like-minded people in our worship experiences—in spite of the fact that all religious organizations are imperfect?

CHAPTER 4

POLITICS MATTERS

If religion is a hard sell for many young people, politics is likely harder. Polls indicate that large numbers of young people are turned off by politics. A *Washington Post* column reported a survey showing that about a quarter of people in the 16–24 age category was even dismissive of democracy. That figure was up from about one-sixth during the 1990s. Younger adults are, unsurprisingly, less likely to vote as evidenced by postelection surveys. This may reflect their greater busyness and unsettled life situations, but there appears to be a fair amount of cynicism about the whole political process.

Reasons for Being "Turned Off" by Politics

Is the widespread political cynicism among young people justified? The deep polarization of American politics in recent decades hardly supports confidence in the public spiritedness of many leaders. Partisan advantage so often eclipses devotion to the common good that the result is political paralysis. It's hard to believe that the polarization is only the effect of high-minded, principled differences of opinion. Democracy has never been a way of avoiding differences; rather, its institutions are designed to manage the inevitable differences in a constructive way. It is supposed to foster civil discourse and help to resolve differences peaceably, but such idealized conceptions of democratic politics do not appear credible when partisan advantage seems more important than the health of a democratic order.

Younger people may be especially "turned off" by the corruption of public officials, not necessarily corruption in terms of bribery or stealing from the public. There are other, fully legal, forms of corruption. For instance, it is quite acceptable for candidates to receive financial contributions. While there are lawful limits to that, in general, campaign contributions are a well-accepted, legal, and necessary aspect of political campaigns. It may be illegal to accept a bribe to support a specific project, but those who have given substantially to a campaign can expect to have a disproportionate influence on the subsequent actions of a winning candidate. That may not be an out-and-out bribe, but it can certainly corrupt the thinking of a public official.

There is also the "revolving door" form of corruption. A public official who has supported the interests of a corporation can sometimes find lucrative employment in that business upon leaving public service. Someone can be corrupted by acting with that prospect in mind. Even if one does not become an employee of the company, one can become a well-paid lobbyist, influencing the political behavior of one's former colleagues in legislative or executive service.

All of this is too widespread to require elaboration. Corruption doesn't have to be grossly illegal; it can take the more subtle form of subordinating the public good for one's own personal interest in getting elected, staying elected, and finding lucrative employment after leaving elective service.

There are other reasons for cynicism. Periodically, a reform movement captures the attention of a younger generation, resulting in widespread action but little success. The 1972 campaign of Senator George McGovern was such a moment. The clearly idealistic Senator McGovern built his campaign on electoral reforms and opposition to the Vietnam War. Large numbers of young people were engaged, contributing time and energy and attending large, enthusiastic rallies. In the end, McGovern lost all but one state (Massachusetts) and the District of Columbia. Many young people became disillusioned.

Similarly, during the 2016 Democratic presidential primary campaign, there was a vast outpouring of support from younger voters for Senator Bernard Sanders. He held huge rallies, enlisted an army of volunteer campaign workers, and raised unprecedented financial contributions. The contributions were far too small to corrupt Sanders, who, in fact, made the role of money in politics a major theme. He won the primaries in many states, although in the end his campaign fell short. Many of his supporters were disillusioned by his defeat, attributing it to a corrupt, rigged process. (That is doubtful, and his opponent, former Secretary of State Hillary Clinton, actually agreed with Sanders on most issues.) The cynicism prompted by the election process is understandable and lingers even today. The victory of President Trump, and its aftermath, did little to diminish cynicism.

Nevertheless, Politics Remains Very Important

There are certainly grounds for cynicism about politics. But does it help? Many of the abuses and corruptions we've spoken of are grounded in human nature, but so is idealism. I like Reinhold Niebuhr's way of speaking of this. Niebuhr pointed out that our "capacity for justice makes democracy possible, [while our] inclination to injustice makes democracy necessary." If people were only selfish by nature, then the political institutions that depend upon public spiritedness could not survive. However, the fact that there's a good deal of self-centeredness in people means that democratic institutions are needed to hold power in check. Sometimes a wave of corruption in politics only reflects widespread moral and spiritual corruption throughout society. The kind of spiritual renewal we referred to in the preceding chapter is relevant to the political order as well as to our personal lives.

Politics matters. To understand this, we need to better understand politics. Politics is about what we all do together: it is about the laws, policies, and actions taken by society acting as a whole. Like it or not, when the state acts, we are all involved. I was personally opposed to the US Vietnam War policy, but my tax dollars still went to support it. This was a fine piece of irony: During that war, I wrote an article opposed to our military involvement that was published in *The Christian Century*. The magazine sent me a payment of about fifty dollars for my article. Part of that went into my federal income tax for the year, some of which actually went to help finance the war! So by writing an article opposed to the war, I was engaged in an economic activity helping to finance it!

Members of some sectarian religious groups, such as the Old Order Amish, don't vote. However, they are deeply engaged in economic activities, thereby increasing the economic base from which taxes are raised. In this way, they are political whether they want to be or not.

So there are ways, some more obvious than others, in which we are all acting together—even in support of governmental actions we don't believe in. An even more extreme illustration of this is how the slaves in the Confederate states were, by raising and picking cotton, increasing the economic basis sustaining the Confederate war effort.

There is no way to avoid being contaminated by what we consider to be wrong in the political order. We can't withdraw into some island of innocence. Whatever the state is doing, we are doing, even if we are rigorously opposed. That should matter to us very much and lead us to express our opposition more effectively.

Politics Determines Outcomes

Many things happen every day that are not determined by political action. But politics has a lot to do with what actually happens on a society-wide basis. There are many examples.

The establishment and maintenance of educational

institutions largely depends on politics. That has not always been so. Until early in the nineteenth century, schools were either private or they were maintained by local communities. The idea of free, mandatory education took hold in many states during the early nineteenth century. Today, that is the policy of all states. While there remain many private schools today, even these are subject to public regulation.

K–12 education is funded by local and state governments, with increasing federal participation. This development was largely pioneered by the United States, although most countries worldwide have adopted this at least in principle. Politics makes education happen on a wide scale and, to a great degree, determines how it will be conducted.

Politics also matters through the public provision of food programs for malnourished and starving children. School-provided lunches and breakfasts for children of impoverished families have become widespread. I still remember the early enactment of some of this. When I was an elementary school-child during the Depression years of the 1930s, we lived in a small southern Ohio town. I remember poor farm children bringing lard sandwiches to school for lunch. It was all their families could afford. Then a New Deal school lunch program began, and these same children received free lunches in the school cafeteria. That was politics in action.

Politics also helped remove stigmas against racial and ethnic groups, girls and women, religious minorities, and, increasingly now, gay and lesbian people. American society has not perfected this trend, but the progress is clear and impressive and a direct result of much political struggle.

So it is with policies to reduce reliance on fossil fuels and contribute to the reduction of global warming. Again the progress is not perfect, but if there had been no political activity, the unrestrained free market would likely not have changed. The provision of health care for everyone—a point at which the United States has lagged behind other industrialized societies—is a goal that will also depend upon public policy. Public policy creates a myriad of regulations governing occupational safety and the safety of food and drugs. In many localities, public policy makes provision for mass transportation, not to mention the obvious creation of a vast network of roads and highways. At national and international levels, policies fostering security and world peace depend primarily on political decision-making. Politics impact us on a deeply personal level.

Laws, rules, and policies about such matters—and many more—don't just happen. They are the result of serious political engagement. Often they become possible only as the result of the dedicated efforts of many public-spirited people. Major reform movements typically take many years. Proponents of change often must endure frequent disappointments. But in the end, political efforts make things happen—some good, some not so good. Whether good or bad, outcomes really do depend on what society does when it acts as a whole through politics.

Politics matters! We've illustrated this mainly with concrete, visible actions, but we shouldn't forget the effect of politics on how people think and the values they live by. Political forces alone do not determine cultural values, but they can have great influence in shaping broadly shared attitudes and values. The civil rights movement and its legislative achievements is one of the best illustrations of this. The Civil Rights Acts of the 1960s were bitterly opposed, but they were largely effective not only in governing actions but also in shaping attitudes. We mustn't overstate that, for much remains to be done; but neither should we ignore the substantial changes that have occurred since the early 1960s. Almost no one today wants to be called a racist; a half century ago, however, many would have taken that as a badge of honor. That is a not-insignificant cultural change. Much of the change, as we noted in the previous chapter, resulted from religious action, but the role of public policy and law also helped.

We Must Not Expect Perfection in Politics

I am not surprised that many young people, having given their all in a great political effort, are disillusioned by recent outcomes. Perhaps it is the defeat of an idealistic candidate or the failure of a leader we supported to follow through. Or even an idealistic candidate who, upon assuming office, is corrupted. Lord Acton was on target with his observation that "power corrupts, and absolute power corrupts absolutely." This is true all too often.

It is not always true, however. There have been high-minded rulers who have had nearly absolute power without being corrupted by it. The first president of the United States could have become king with enormous power and no term limit. He is supposed to have remarked that, while his own inauguration as president was significant, the most important inauguration would be that of his successor, for that act would clearly establish the precedent of a peaceful transfer of power. So Washington demonstrated that great power does not necessarily corrupt.

Also, though politics is not perfect, remember that in a well-organized democratic state, there are counterbalances to diminish corruption, even if they don't eliminate it completely. In such states, holders of power face an opposition also in power; and, as President Washington anticipated, power *can* be limited in time.

It is an illusion to expect politics to illustrate and yield perfection. Human beings are not perfect. You and I are not perfect. Social interactions are not perfect. Institutions are not perfect. So politics is not perfect. The best way to avoid disillusionment is not to have too many illusions in the first place.

The Importance of Compromise

I can understand why those with important political goals, grounded in their deepest values, are wary of compromise. The very word conjures up a sense of "selling out" our integrity. But let's look at compromise more closely. Only rarely can we achieve everything we hope for in politics. We're not even always right! (Moral righteousness can drift into self-righteousness.) In addition, the views of our political adversaries may not be all bad. At the very least, they hold some political power that cannot be wished away—and not always voted away either.

It is true, however, that some compromises are better than others. I don't believe we should compromise our basic principles by publicly disavowing them. We shouldn't call a good thing bad or a bad thing good. At the same time, we can respect the principles held by others even if we don't share them. Where we might consider other principles wrong-headed or even dishonest, we may have to compromise with their power. Suppose you are interested in increasing local funding for much-needed improvements in school facilities (students are relegated to subpar temporary classrooms). The need seems obvious to you. Others are equally concerned about homelessness in your city, including a number of homeless families with children. Both needs are real, but the local budget is already strained, and there isn't enough money to give to both groups. Could you support a compromise where both sides receive part but not all of what they need? That kind of compromise is often faced when legislative bodies—from local to national levels—work on funding issues. Rarely can all needs be met fully, even with tax increases.

Compromises of this sort are not unusual in legislative bodies or even in nonpolitical settings. A local church budget or the budget of a labor union or a community center will likely confront competing needs. A willingness to compromise can often move things along. *Sometimes we must be content with incremental gains, looking toward future progress.* That can be true even when we are facing opponents whose objectives are, in our view, without merit.

What About Political Parties?

A growing number of Americans have decided it is wrong, even morally wrong, to affiliate with a political party. Recent studies (by Gallup and Pew) put the number of self-identified independents at around 40 percent, more than either the Republican or Democratic parties—although a majority of these independents regularly support one or the other of the major parties. No doubt, motivations vary widely. One widespread perception is that political parties seem to invite corruption and create unholy alliances among very different interest groups.

Voters registered as independents played an important role in the 2016 presidential election. An appreciable number of voters registered with minor parties, such as the Libertarian and Green Parties, as a protest against the major Republican and Democratic Parties. Turning toward the independent option can be a reaction against the imperfections—even corruptions—of major parties.

However, even though registering as an independent can appear to be the more ethical, uncompromising option, the current political reality is that you exert the greatest influence by registering and participating in one of the major parties. When you are actively engaged in a major political party, you are in a better position to be heard. I don't want to overstate the point, but it does seem clear that participants generally have more influence than bystanders.

Also, we should always vote. If we don't vote, we are, in effect, endorsing the winner—whether we like it or not. Not voting weakens the fabric of democracy. We should consider participation, especially through voting, to be a sacred duty because politics matters, elections matter, voting matters, and democracy matters.

A Note to Younger Readers

We must grasp that the political order involves all of us acting together, whether we like it or not. I have listed several important outcomes of the political process. What are others—both good and bad? We all have some degree of political power, small or large. Do these facts about politics suggest ways we can be more effective? Is this a responsibility growing out of our deepest moral commitments?

CHAPTER 5

COMMUNITY MATTERS

As Aristotle said, we are by nature social animals. We belong to one another, not just for convenience or to use one another, but because social relationships are essential to our humanity.

Community vs. Competition

Not everybody believes that. A great debate, worldwide in scope, is currently raging between those who think of society as a sphere of self-interested competition and those who see it as a community of mutual caring. The poet T. S. Eliot put the issue succinctly in these words:

When the Stranger says: "What is the meaning of this city?

Do you huddle close together because you love each
    other?"
What will you answer? "We all dwell together
To make money from each other"? or "This is a
    community"?

We should never settle for that first response, even
though in our economic life we do depend upon mutual
trade. Treating one another only as a source of economic
gain, though, dehumanizes others and, in the process, dehumanizes us as well.

A number of years ago, a group of my students and I
studied farm labor conditions in southern Florida. That took
us to Belle Glade, a town in the orange-growing area. One
early morning, we visited the labor pool area where workers
lined up looking for work for the day. Labor bosses looked
them over, talking with each other about how many "head"
of workers they needed. The term, similar to how they might
have spoken about "head of cattle," suggested unmistak-
ably that these workers were not fellow human beings. They
were only so many units of money-making productivity to be
hired or discarded at will. Even now, a common HR term is
human capital, referring to employees.

Similarly, corporations speak of their fiduciary obligation

to stockholders as though that is the sole criterion of success or failure. The term *fiduciary responsibility* often refers to the good faith effort by business leaders to place the interests of stockholders above their own. Under the law, this means avoiding conflicts of interest. Unspoken, of course, is the actual goal of enhancing the wealth and income of corporate officials. Even when conflicts of interest are avoided, fiduciary responsibility frequently ignores the well-being of other stakeholders—like the employees, the environment, or society as a whole—unless there is external pressure that cannot be ignored. (Responsibility to the customer is taken into account, but that is to maximize corporate income.)

I don't want to press this point too hard because there are corporations with a good sense of their responsibilities to the whole community. But the narrower view is represented in a good deal of economic literature: The Austrian and Chicago schools of economic thought, featuring Friedrich von Hayek, Ludwig von Mises, and Milton Friedman, emphasize market freedom as the great engine of productivity and, in the long run, of social well-being. They have echoed the pioneer economist Adam Smith, who, in *The Wealth of Nations*, emphasized that if all economic actors sought only their own self-interest, the "hidden hand" of the market would best serve everyone.

There is an element of truth in Smith's words, but not much.

This model of economic life has a tendency to leave many in poverty. Even if Smith and his modern economic echoes were entirely right, the main point about our being human in and through community would be lost. We are economic beings, of course. We have economic needs that must be met, and human economic creativity can benefit us all. However, we are first of all social beings. Economics should benefit the community because the quality of community life really does matter.

The Personal Dimension

We are most likely to think of community as we experience it in small groups and person-to-person relationships. Somebody dies. Immediately, neighbors bring food and flowers, reaching out with sympathy. We've mentioned that kind of personal contact within churches, but such community is not limited to religious settings. It may be most evident in small towns, but it can also be experienced in large cities. For many years my family lived in a very large city, but we would have block parties on our street. Parents would help raise each other's kids like local versions of the theme of Hillary Clinton's book *It Takes a Village*. From a young person's viewpoint, community is expressed through relationships with playmates. Sometimes these relationships last a lifetime.

We also create community online through Facebook and other social networking sites. People of my age sometimes wonder whether such contacts are too impersonal. Can you really get to know people you never actually meet face-to-face? Well, yes. I suspect some of the so-called impersonal internet connections can in fact become very personal as people learn a lot about one another through repeated and frequent interactions. I believe this dimension of community will sort itself out over time. In the meantime, my advice to younger people is not to rely upon internet connections as their sole means of relating to others. In that respect, I sympathize with parents who seek to limit the time their children spend in this way, encouraging them to invest more in face-to-face relationships and in their studies and outdoor activities. But internet connections, such as Facebook, are doubtless here to stay. Our objective must be a balance in our forms of relationships.

Schools and colleges can be thriving communities, too. It may be hard in state universities with tens of thousands of students or in high schools with two or three thousand students, but even such settings can provide a community focus. This is likely most evident in the school spirit evoked by athletic events or other special occasions. Even in large schools and colleges, there are usually subgroups where lasting friendships are born. The sense of community can be even more vibrant in smaller schools and colleges. My own undergraduate years were spent in a small California college of about one thousand students. In my graduate years, I attended Boston University with, at that time, approximately twenty thousand students. Both offered important forms of community, though both were quite different.

From our earliest days, we are involved in all sorts of community relationships that are deeply humanizing. Such relationships matter more than we realize.

Community and Culture

Our relationships within the community are culturally defined and expressed. We have inherited language, traditions, ways of acting and believing. Our involvement in our inherited culture begins very early in life and continues to grow as long as we live. Much of this is taken in and expressed without thought. We add or subtract from the culture both through our creative contributions and decisions but also through what we support or reject. If community matters, then the cultural contents through which community is expressed matter as well.

Shared cultural views and practices can be either good

or bad. During my childhood years in a small Ohio town, racism was in the very air we breathed. Racist jokes were tossed off with shared laughter—among whites, of course—and the racist minstrel shows were common. On the radio, many enjoyed the *Amos 'n' Andy* programs with demeaning stereotypes of African Americans. I am grateful that my own family was largely resistant to such cultural currents, but that was the general reality. On the other hand, it really matters that publicly displayed or voiced racism is no longer generally acceptable in American culture. That doesn't mean that racism no longer exists, but it does mean that it is widely rejected in the culture. Similar points could be made about other cultural attitudes and practices. The struggle between positive and negative aspects of culture is ongoing.

It matters whether or not we devote ourselves to those aspects of culture that are good and beautiful and ennobling. In our social relationships, we can help to deepen the quality of community life by our choices of what to emphasize from inherited culture and what we attend to in the cultural expressions of our times. We can pay serious attention to the arts, to works of history and biography, to literature that explores the human tradition, either in fictional or nonfictional form. Our exposure to cultural treasures can occur through formal education, but it is a lifelong pursuit.

Facing Crises Together

The beauty of community is especially experienced during times of crisis. Isn't it striking how people who seem indifferent to others will rally around when confronted by disaster? A house catches fire. Neighbors rush to call the fire department, sometimes even risking their own lives to save the occupants. An earthquake, flood, or hurricane strikes a town or city. People react as one to the catastrophe, quite unselfishly helping one another. Catastrophic hurricanes and wildfire events offer many well-publicized examples. A big snowfall paralyzes a city. It is not particularly life-threatening, but it is a shared inconvenience. Life comes to a standstill. For a few hours or days, people feel their oneness with others.

A striking aspect of the 9/11 catastrophe in New York, Washington, and Pennsylvania was how people were drawn together. In New York, many people helped out, some heroically. In such times of crisis, many people experience their humanity in deeper levels. That may be most evident in battlefield settings. Combatants often report later how intense this was, noting they were especially concerned about the well-being of their immediate comrades. Sometimes the safety and survival of fellow soldiers transcended even the common cause for which they were fighting.

71

The intensity of crisis, often bringing out the best in us, suggests that there are latent bonds of community all along. It just takes a crisis to bring them out. Some people do react selfishly or indifferently even in the presence of great human suffering around them, but isn't it beautiful when neighbors and communities come together to share the burden of loss and rebuild their homes and lives?

Wider Dimensions of Community

Face-to-face experiences of community are most immediate to all of us. Without these, our humanity is diminished. Community is also present at national and even global levels. Waves of patriotism are an expression of community, linking us to vast numbers of people we will never know personally.

During World War II, the populations of the United States and other countries were drawn together in common purpose. In the United States, this was referred to as the home front. People supported the war effort in various ways, including buying war bonds to help finance the effort. That was a pretelevision era, but news was avidly consumed from newspapers, radios, and newscasts in movie theaters. People displayed flags and little banners in their windows with blue stars showing how many soldiers or sailors from their family were serving. If one died in service, the blue star was replaced with a gold one. People were linked to perfect strangers as fellow Americans.

At the end of the war, the global community came together. Determined not to repeat the failures of the earlier League of Nations, there was a great outpouring of support for a new United Nations organization. The imagery and rhetoric accompanying this effort appealed to a common sense of humanity. We were one with the people of Asia, Africa, and Europe. Even the defeated Germans and Japanese were ultimately included. The sense of global unity transcended nationalism.

While global unity cannot involve personal contact with everyone, the interesting thing is that it affects how we interact with people of other nations and cultures when we do meet them. When we travel to other countries, we will inevitably find ourselves in contact with strangers. How do we experience them? Are they alien to us? Or are there bonds of fellow humanity that come quickly to the surface?

In the 1970s, during the Cold War between the United States and Soviet Bloc countries of eastern Europe, my family was on a camping trip in Europe. We met many people who were friendly and helpful, but most striking was when we drove our VW microbus from Berlin across East Germany to Czechoslovakia, which was an alien territory. At the Czech border, we were in a long line of bumper-to-bumper traffic, moving at a snail's pace. Behind us, several cars started honking. Opening the window to see what was the matter, we saw several people pointing to the rear of our vehicle. Smoke was pouring out of our engine. As we investigated, we discovered that oil was leaking onto a hot surface, causing the smoke. Someone offered chewing gum for a (very) temporary plug. The border guards were helpful even though we were obviously American.

Later, in Prague, we had a hard time finding our campground. A taxi driver, seeing our problem, volunteered to guide us and wouldn't accept any compensation. That act expressed the bonds of community, reaching above all of the international tensions existing between the United States and Soviet Bloc countries. Over the next days, we experienced such friendship with others. During future trips to Kenya, the Philippines, Costa Rica, Malaysia, India, and New Zealand, we experienced the same outpouring of kindness and humanity.

As I write these words, there are other deep tensions throughout the world. Humanity is undercut by terrorism and profound interreligious challenges. I am particularly disturbed by new waves of economic nationalism. Are we doomed to

T. S. Eliot's picture of interacting only to make money from each other? Or even worse, to exploit each other?

Many economists have long since concluded that trade wars and national protectionism are formulas for hardship not for gain. Economically, we need trade relationships encouraging productivity everywhere for the benefit of all the world's people. But more than that, economics exists as a means to a greater end—the goal of human well-being. An element of competition in the open market may help, but the world cannot be made up of winners and losers. In community, if there are any losers, we are all losers.

Barriers to Community

Given the value of community life, why is it so difficult to achieve? In part, it is in conflict with ordinary selfishness and issues we've noted already, but there are two other barriers that often stand in the way.

The first of these is excessive inequality. Some inequality is inevitable partly because of the differences among human beings. For instance, some people are physically stronger than others and thus are more capable of many forms of physical work. Roughly half the human race is more capable than the other half of bearing children. All human beings have brains, but some are more gifted than others in different forms of intelligence—though it goes without saying that all types of intelligence are a gift to the community. We all benefit from the rich panoply of human gifts, with the different kinds of contributions people make to the common good.

Inequality, though, can still be a barrier. Some people lack the resources to be full participants in community life. Some may be denied equal political rights. A repressive regime will divide a society between its supporters and its opponents, and the kinds of rights embedded in the US Constitution's Bill of Rights will be discarded. That threatens human interactions at many levels. Even when gross lack of human resources and the loss of human rights are not a problem, some people may be treated as having more worth than others. When I look up to someone more than I do to others, or when I look down on someone, it interferes with our interactions as fellow human beings.

Historically, the other barrier to community in the United States has been more serious. The original sin of American communal life, virtually from the beginning, has been racism. Slavery has been practiced in human society from time immemorial, often when slaves were drawn from the losers in war, but slavery in the United States represented the capturing and enslavement of people from Africa. The extraordinary evil of this act was compounded by how people of African descent were defined as inherently inferior, even less than fully human. One of the worst expressions I ever encountered was in a letter written by a mid-twentieth-century Methodist bishop from Texas. The bishop wrote that he had always considered African Americans (he called them Negroes) as "pre-Adamic." What does that mean? The bishop thought that the biblical Adam was the first-created human being. Anything before that wasn't fully human! Perhaps those who were "pre-Adamic" were part of an evolutionary sequence, but real human beings were not.

Such racism, whether in its crudest or more moderate forms, has been a huge barrier to real community in America. The Jim Crow laws and customs that took hold after the Civil War and abolition of slavery perpetuated walls of separation in this country, often enforced with savage brutality. Even more recently, after a number of African American men were shot by police around 2013, a movement developed with the slogan "Black Lives Matter." The point was that the lives of these victims were valuable and would not have been lost had they not been African American. An immediate response from numbers of individuals was that "All Lives Matter," not just African Americans. But critics of the movement's slogan missed the point. Our culture has largely always affirmed

77

the value of white lives; it has often treated black people as having less value or no value at all. A chain is no stronger than its weakest link, and the chain of human value has been at its weakest in respect to the treatment of black people. To single out black lives in this way is to focus on the point where American culture and community has been weakest and proven a barrier to true community in this country.

Being Both Individual and Social

Does this emphasis on community mean that we are *only* social? Does Aristotle's comment about our being social by nature mean that we are only parts of a social whole? Some of the ideological debates of the last couple of centuries have implied that we have to choose one or the other. The philosopher/novelist Ayn Rand saw us in purely individualistic terms. One of her books even bore the title *The Virtue of Selfishness*. The writings of some economists, like Milton Friedman, without going quite that far, did seem to think of us primarily as individuals. On the other hand, writings influenced by Karl Marx and other socialists have tended to speak of us in primarily, if not exclusively, communitarian terms. That is, of course, the point of the Fascists.

Both extremes, the purely individualistic and the purely

social, are only half truths. The real point is you cannot have one without the other. Society, the community, depends upon individuals who are creative, purposeful, caring selves. Individuals are sustained, nurtured, and humanized by community. Great creative minds—the Beethovens, the Rembrandts, the Aristotles, the Alcotts, the Carvers—are fully individual; however, the expressions of their creative genius draw inspiration from community and are given back to community. Their sense of selfhood is both individual and communal.

All of us possess the capacity to be creative individuals, drawing our personhood from community and rendering back the gifts we have to bring to the common table.

A Note to Younger Readers

We are both individual and social by nature. We cannot be fully human without being involved in community—so community matters. We've illustrated this in various ways, noting the importance of culture and our growth in learning from its deepest insights and beauties.

CHAPTER 6

FAMILY MATTERS

We owe our very lives to family. No matter how the conception and birth came to be, whether traditionally or through an alternative path, we cannot survive as human beings without receiving nurturing care for at least the earliest years of life—and probably considerably more. Families take many forms, but even if it is limited to a single mother and child, it is indisputably necessary for survival.

Being Nurtured Badly or Well

Sometimes we are cared for very well; other times rather badly. Some families are unfortunately dysfunctional, even abusive. A fair number of teenagers and adults look back on their early years with pain. Working through the effects of a damaged childhood can take a lifetime; sometimes it never quite comes together. Tragically, dysfunctional, abusive parents are simply repeating what happened to them, so the pattern is often repeated generation after generation.

That doesn't have to be the case! I don't know how you'd measure this statistically, but my impression is that a large majority of families aren't all that bad. Teenagers can feel that their parents are not very understanding or are even too harsh. I find it interesting that later these same people will reassess those early years more positively, as in, "My mom and dad really were pretty good." It's not so unusual that relationships between parents and children are strained during the teen years. It can even be necessary as adolescents form their independent identities. Grandparents often view this dynamic with amusement when their own children complain about grandchildren. "Ah," we might say, "your kids are just like you were!" Despite the tensions, nurturing our families well through the years is critical to forming life-giving relationships.

Commitment Matters

Regardless of different forms of family life and tensions that may appear in relationships, it matters whether family members are committed to one another. This is a crucial aspect of love. Commitment is possible even in the most extreme situations. Haven't we seen instances of family members sticking with each other even when one has committed a horrible crime—like a mass killing in a school or on the streets? Other family members are in shocked disbelief and profoundly embarrassed. They cannot and will not excuse what happened, but they do not abandon their commitment, their love, to this family member. They may feel the weight of earlier failures—there's no turning back on that—but neither will they demonize the one they love.

I'm also struck by another phenomenon. Very often, divorced parents, who once committed themselves "for better or worse...until death do us part," continue to affirm that commitment in relation to their children—sometimes even fighting over custody. There is something inextinguishable about the parent-child relationship, even when the warmth of marriage has been extinguished.

Family is where the deeper values of committed love are nourished and sustained. It is where we embrace one another despite imperfections and disappointments. It is where we are best known, even as we know others in their gifts and flaws. An old Arabian proverb, speaking of friendship, puts it this way: "A friend is one to whom you can pour out all the contents of your heart, chaff and grain together, knowing that the gentlest of hands will take and sift it, keep what is worth keeping and, with the breath of kindness, blow the rest away." We don't always measure up to that standard in our family relationships, but it matters that we keep trying.

New Developments in Family Life

What is the best form of family? I don't believe anyone is in a position to say! Occasionally, a more conservative Christian will say we should return to the biblical view. But which one? Would it be the polygamous marriages of Abraham or of King David and King Solomon (which are cited with approval in the Old Testament)? Would it be the judgment of the apostle Paul, who encouraged his readers not to get married unless they could not control their sexual impulses? Would it be the father/mother/children model? Most Christians who speak of the biblical example plainly have this latter one in mind. That has, in fact, been the dominant pattern in most countries for a very long time. It can be described as traditional marriage.

Traditional marriage is not for everyone; it never has been. Still, we need deep, enduring relationships, grounded in mutual commitments made "for better or worse"—not only for our own well-being but to enable the creation of future generations. It might appear that much is being put to the test.

During the 1970s, traditionally minded people were shocked by the emergence of communes in which free sex marked relationships. Physical relationships dominated without mutual commitments. Perhaps predictably, these forms of family—if they could be called that—have largely passed away. They simply did not fulfill the human need to give and receive love.

The failure of the communes, however, did not mean a wholesale return to traditional marriage relationships. There continued to be a fair amount of casual sexual activity and even monogamous relationships outside of formal, legal marriage. I can report, from my own pastoral experience during the 1990s, that something like 90 percent of the many wedding ceremonies I performed were for couples who had already been living with each other, often for several years. In conversation with other pastors, I discovered that that was a widespread pattern. It reminded me of the late philosopher Bertrand Russell's advocacy of trial marriage. I don't stand in judgment of those premarital relationships, although I'm skeptical that such a pattern will endure over the long run. For one thing, if the breakup of such unions is one-sided, the other party is going to be hurt. For another, something is missing in this most intimate relationship if commitment is missing. I could be wrong. It seems to me that it is one of those vast social experiments that will either succeed over the long run or fail and pass away. It is something the younger generation will have to work out in its own way.

Another dimension of modern-day family life is divorce. It is widespread. When divorce is caused by abuse (usually of the wife by the husband), one can only say that such a union is not a real marriage. For centuries, Christian churches, both Catholic and Protestant, strongly disapproved of divorce. Even today, the official Catholic position is that the church will not recognize the remarriage of a divorced person. The one exception is if the marriage has been annulled, which means that it is regarded as never having been a real marriage at all. Tribunals in that church have been established to examine and certify that a divorce was really of that kind. That can lead to an element of fiction, of course. Most Protestant churches now allow for remarriage, though I can still remember when my Methodist denomination would only do so if it could be established that the person desiring remarriage was not the one responsible for the divorce. The psychological absurdity of such a provision finally led my church to abandon the effort to say who was guilty or not. It remains that divorce is evidence of a failure and often of a great deal of hurt—and sometimes much bitterness. The real victims of divorce tend to be children who may entertain fantasies for years of reuniting their parents. I still believe it best for couples to enter into marriage with the full intention of sticking with it. Many couples have discovered that commitment can see them through rough places in their relationship, often discovering their relationship is better afterward.

As we consider new patterns of family relationship, a third development is the emerging phenomenon of gay and lesbian marriage. There has been a huge change in public opinion about same-gender marriage within a few years, with recent polls showing that more than 60 percent of Americans now accept it. This is partly due to increased recognition that homosexuality is not simply a choice people make; rather, it is a condition they come to recognize about themselves, earlier or later. I believe widespread opposition to same-gender marriage was largely, if unconsciously, based on the perception that a gay or lesbian lifestyle was inherently promiscuous. If true, this is ironic, for committed marriage is a step away from promiscuity. The US Supreme Court's decision legalizing same-gender marriage expressed this eloquently in Justice Anthony Kennedy's words:

> No union is more profound than marriage, for it embodies the highest ideals of love, fidelity, devotion, sacrifice, and family. In forming a marital union, two

people become something greater than once they were. . . . It would misunderstand these [homosexual] men and women to say they disrespect the idea of marriage. Their plea is that they do respect it, respect it so deeply that they seek to find its fulfillments for themselves. Their hope is not to be condemned to live in loneliness, excluded from one of civilization's oldest institutions.

Those words, from the secular Supreme Court, affirm the importance of commitment in all marriage.

We All Need Deep, Enduring Relationships

Traditional marriage may not be for everyone, though it will likely continue to be for most. Regardless of whether or not one gets married and forms a family, though, we all need intimate relationships of mutual caring. That may not be so obvious in young adult years, but as the years pass by, having such relationships becomes more and more important. This is partly because mutual care-giving matters more as we grow older. Even more importantly, we need to feel we are loved and that it will never end. Most of us also need to have one to whom we can give love in that deeper, enduring sense.

Besides a partner, children can be a large part of deep, enduring relationships. The majority of people are likely to form traditional families and have children. Even if we don't bring new life into the world, though, we have much to gain from bonded relationships with children. Many lifelong singles who have never married, whether by choice or circumstance, can still form and nurture relationships with children that are wholesome and life-giving. Numbers of gay and lesbian couples are adopting infants or small children because of their wish to provide that nurturing relationship. For all who invest themselves in the care of children, it is the beginning of a lifelong adventure: caring for the children through their early years, watching in wonderment as they grow, navigating the difficulties of rebellion, and mentoring along the way without impeding maturing independence. Toward the end of life, you then see they are there for you as you have been there for them. The rewards that come with having children (and later having grandchildren) are a tremendous gift despite the difficulties encountered through the many days, months, and years of relationship.

Whatever the form of "family," it won't work perfectly. We're all too human for that! Problems can surface in broken marital relationships, in the relationship between parents and children, and between siblings themselves. Often these are tragic evidences of human brokenness. We have all known siblings who have sustained bitter relationships for many years. Sometimes the issues have to do with money, sometimes just the nurtured remembrance of early childhood tensions. My counsel to anyone who still holds onto old hostilities is to work hard to move through them, even taking the first step. So much is at stake in the long run.

And whatever the form it takes, at the root of family is love and commitment. Robert Frost said: "Home is where, when you have to go there, they have to take you in." That speaks of the quality of commitment and the sense of belonging that comes with families.

Cultural Barriers to Healthy Family Life

Despite the importance of healthy family life, there continue to be aspects of inherited culture that stand in the way. I think especially of inherited sexism, some of which is even affirmed in parts of the Christian New Testament. It is not surprising that there have been some role differences between men and women historically, but even when appropriate to a preindustrial ages, the differences have never justified relationships of dominance and subservience. It has become much easier to see that in the industrial and postindustrial age, where physical strength is much less important economically and where many labor-saving devices in the home have liberated women from chores that seemed, but never were, less important than typical male roles in the workplace.

I co-officiated a wedding ceremony some years ago with a more biblically conservative fellow clergyman. In his homily, he selected the following passage from the New Testament Book of Ephesians: "Wives, be subject to your husbands as you are to the Lord. For the husband is the head of the wife just as Christ is the head of the church, the body of which he is the Savior. Just as the church is subject to Christ, so also wives ought to be, in everything, to their husbands" (5:22–24).

Uh oh, I thought. *Will those lines define the wedding?* I had known the bride since her infancy; while she was a fairly conservative Christian, I knew she was also something of a feminist. In his homily that immediately followed, however, the other minister said he had chosen this passage deliberately because it was so often misunderstood to mean the husband's dominance of the wife. That wasn't what it meant at all, he said. Rather, it was about the husband's responsibility to protect and care for his wife. As an analogy, he spoke of a flock of geese in their shaped formation, with one goose in front, breaking the air currents for the geese that followed.

Whether or not that was true to the meaning of Ephesians,

I found it helpful to relieve the patriarchal images. After the service, however, I approached my colleague with a question: Is it always the same goose in front of the V-formation? Wouldn't fatigue set in? Wouldn't other geese take their turn up front? And isn't that a better analogy for marriage, with each partner carrying a share of the responsibility? The other minister readily agreed.

In fact, that isn't a bad analogy for a family as a whole. We all have different roles to play. A wife and husband may, over time, switch roles. I can recall periods when I handled the family financial responsibilities and times when my wife, Carolyn, took over. Through most of the years, she did most of the cooking; in our later years, I've begun to prepare breakfast and we let our retirement center prepare dinner. Some things she is better fitted to do, while at other points—such as shoveling snow and making repairs to the house—I am better fitted to do. Wise parents even put their children to work in age-appropriate ways. All of this worked rather well in the farm families of a now-receding past. Men did the plowing, women did the cooking, and children had their chores, like milking the cows and bringing in the eggs.

In a healthy family, no one dominates oppressively. Children grow and learn through family nurture. It is where they absorb the most important lessons about life in community. School years become very important, of course, but the family supports and supplements what is learned in school in very important ways. And, it must be added, parents learn a whole lot from their children!

A Note to Younger Readers

You wouldn't be here without having parents, regardless of the form the parenting took. I have sought to emphasize in this chapter that stable, loving family life helps us grow from infancy to maturity. Such family life is based on enduring commitments of parents to each other (where that is possible), of parents to children, and of siblings to each other. We cannot know how family life will evolve in coming years, but loving commitment has great lasting power.

CHAPTER 7

VOCATION MATTERS

The importance of vocation came to me one day from an unexpected place. Checking into a New Jersey hotel a few years ago, I found a card on a table in our room. It contained these words:

TO OUR GUESTS

Because this hotel is a human institution to serve people, and not solely a money-making organization, we hope that God will grant you peace and rest while you are under our roof. May this room and hotel be your "second home." ... We are all travelers. From birth 'til death we travel between eternities. May these days be pleasant for you, profitable for society, helpful for those you meet, and a joy to those who know and love you best.

The message conveyed the management's own sense of vocation. It was also a challenge to their guests to have a similar sense about the importance of our lives and our impact upon others. In a large sense, this is what vocation is really about—and why it matters.

The word *vocation* comes from the Latin *vocare*, which means "to call." Originally, vocation had to do with what you were called to do. In the Christian church, it originally meant being called by God to be a priest, monk, or nun, engaged specifically in church work. In more recent centuries, particularly in Protestant Christian settings, the term has been broadened to include any "life's work" to which one feels a divine call.

Martin Luther, who flourished five hundred years ago, was the first major figure to register this point. He wrote, "A cobbler, a smith, a farmer, each has the work and office of his trade, and yet they are all alike consecrated priests and bishops, and every one by means of his own work or office must benefit and serve every other." And, "What you do in your house is worth as much as if you did it up in heaven for our Lord God....We should accustom ourselves to think of our position and work as sacred and well-pleasing to God." To Luther, the work to which we are called is based on our inherited station in life. The son of a peasant farmer would expect to be a peasant farmer. The daughter of a peasant farmer would expect to be a mother and keeper of the home. A person born into any station, however, could be called to be a priest or nun, but this was not the majority.

The reformer John Calvin also considered secular work to be a calling, although he had a broader sense of how one might not be limited to an inherited station in life. He believed one could be called to be a farmer, a teacher, a doctor or nurse, or a lawyer—yes, even a lawyer. One's calling was a sacred duty, one's way of serving God and fellow humanity. Of course, that did not mean everything you did was vocational. This idea is conveyed at the entrance to the Interchurch Center in New York City, where there is a carved mural depicting a variety of occupations and bearing the words, "Whatever you do, do all to the glory of God." One could be engaged in other activities, but this vocation was one's primary focus for most of one's lifetime. And in a religious sense, it could be devoted to divine purposes even if not in the context of institutional religion.

That largely Protestant idea of vocation is not widely accepted by people today, partly because it is a religious idea, partly because it has lost its moral roots, and partly because what was seen as having deeper meaning has now largely been reduced to making a living. It has become exceedingly difficult to sustain a sense of life as vocation. Mundane life is often stripped of religious meaning, but it doesn't have to be. What we do with our days matters, and vocation helps guide our steps.

A Sense of Calling Can Be Misguided

What we accept as a calling from God can be anything but. Note, for example, the deep sense of God's calling that was expressed vividly by King James I of England as he proclaimed the divine right of kings: "The state of monarchy is the supremest thing on earth; for kings are not only God's lieutenants upon earth, and sit upon God's throne, but even by God himself are called gods." That, to be sure, is just about the limit of human pretentiousness in identifying one's work or status as divinely given! But I can think of more recent political figures who consider it their divine calling to enact legislation that compels adherence to their own narrow commitments.

People can also feel called to a line of work for which they are ill suited. We may be inspired by the example of some great artist, athlete, or scientist and feel called to follow their example even though we lack the talent or self-discipline to succeed in that work. I will say more about this below, but a true sense of vocation must be linked to realistic possibilities. That wouldn't have been much of a problem in the late medieval world. If you were born into a peasant family—as most were—you could wind up as a pretty good farmer. Similarly, if you were the son of a cobbler, carpenter, or stone mason, you'd probably be well fitted to follow in your father's footsteps. Through many centuries, if you were a girl, you would aspire to be like your mother—the only question was whether you would find a proper husband.

The world is vastly different today than in medieval times. People today cannot simply assume they have the capacity to pursue what they may feel called to do. I was, for many years, a seminary professor, which means I had numerous conversations with seminary students about their calling to ministry. While the form of the calling varied greatly, most students seemed authentic to me—both in their motivation and in their realism about their capacities. Now and then someone would express a deep, heartfelt calling that was, in balance, completely unrealistic. So we considered it to be one of the seminary's responsibilities to help such students come to terms with what they could and should do.

I knew a student once who decided as an early teen that he was called to ministry. He followed that path through high school and college. It was only after a few months of seminary that he realized that was *not* what he should be doing. He discovered that, instead, his real calling was to be a school superintendent—a position in which he was highly successful. This student's earlier decision to prepare for ministry had been largely prompted by the fact that his father was a minister. Following in a parent's footsteps can sometimes be the right move, but not always. Young people can sometimes feel pressure in that direction. My word to parents is not to treat your children as an extension of your own life and career. The unique individuality of every child should be respected. My word to children is not to let parental pressure influence you unduly. You have your own life to live.

Discerning Our True Vocation

Basic vocational decisions can take time. A young person can realistically contemplate several possibilities, each of them appealing. I recall weighing the relative appeal of careers in high school history teaching, law, and even music. I could probably have made either the teaching or legal options work, but most certainly not the music. If anything, the career options today are much less clear, partly because of technological and economic changes and partly because specific roles are less defined.

Vocational discernment may not take shape during the childhood years either. Children are frequently asked what they want to be when they grow up. Often the answer will be something like, "I want to be a fireman." That is a viable career option, but society can employ only a limited number of firefighters. For various reasons, that childhood wish may easily change as the years go by. (But it is, of course, a good thing that there are people who follow that path.)

Given that vocational discernment can take time, on what basis should young people make vocational choices? First, the decision should not be made on the basis of money. Income is a necessity for most people, but money as a driving motivation is not consistent with the idea of vocation. There are likely exceptions to that. I almost think the contemporary multibillionaire Warren Buffett might be one. He is a genius at making money through investing, but he doesn't hoard money. In fact, Buffett has expressed a desire to use his wealth for the good of society. Recognizing that he lacks the talent to make wise decisions about philanthropy, he turned most of those decisions over to the Gates Foundation. Even John Wesley, founder of Methodism, advocated that his followers should work all they could to gain all they could, but he added: so they could *give* all they could. He earned large sums of money through the sale of his books. But he lived a fairly Spartan lifestyle, using his income in service to the poor and in support of the movement. For most people, maximizing income is not a goal that is consistent with true vocation.

Second, the primary consideration in discerning vocation should be the good to be accomplished. For believers, that would be something like the views of Luther or Calvin: pour your life energies into advancing the purposes of God on earth as best you understand them. For those who don't share that faith in a purposeful God, it can at least mean contributing to the well-being of humanity and the enhancement of the natural world. None of us can accomplish everything that needs to be done, but each of us can use our unique gifts, blended with those of other people, to accomplish something.

A third consideration in vocational discernment is our inclinations. What do we *want* to do with our lives? How can we be most creative? In the broadest sense, what would be most fun? A searching question here is whether we could sustain the hard, disciplined (and sometimes boring) work that most serious vocations entail. If your gift is music, you'll have to spend countless hours mastering the violin or piano, for example, when you'd just as soon be doing something else. If you're a writer, similar effort must go into that work, often subjecting your work to constant rewriting. If you're an electrician or plumber, you'll have to go through a good deal of apprenticeship to acquire the skills and abilities to do your job with excellence. Your desire to do a chosen form of work must be strong enough to endure the least pleasant but necessary work that goes with it.

A fourth consideration for discerning vocation is our actual giftings. Can we really do what we would like to do and do it on a level that will make a contribution? You may have a personal sense of that, but it is a good idea to consult with people who know you and the chosen field well. This may be a teacher, a mentor, career counselors, or somebody involved in the field. There are also various vocational aptitude tests. Advisors may not always be right, but you are not alone in your decision.

Fifth, it is wise to consider the likely opportunities in the chosen field. This is partly an economic factor and partly a matter of limited spaces—there may be too few openings for too many talented people. For instance, I'm told that the number of aspiring actors greatly exceeds the space in Broadway plays or movies. In part, this may also come down to sheer luck—being discovered, being at the right place at the right time.

Above all else, the true test of vocation, ultimately, is whether the work we do in our chosen field is in the service of love. For Christians this is really clear. I believe it is also the final test for those who do not share Christian faith. Do we love humanity? Do we love the natural world, gifted to us through vast millennia of time? Are we engaging in our work wholeheartedly, that is, with our whole heart, in the service of love? These are not abstract ethical questions, although our thinking may largely be abstract.

These same considerations can govern our decisions regardless of how many times we make changes in our career. Our motivation remains, essentially, the same: loving service. We must expect circumstances and opportunities to change, but the general direction of our life work may serve as a kind of vocational compass.

Thinking About Our "Sub-Vocations"

Our life's work is not all that matters. As important as it is, our chosen vocation is not where we spend all of our time and energy. Aren't there other aspects of life that can be chosen and pursued in a vocational spirit? We can refer to these as sub-vocations. They may not involve as much of our time as the broader vocation, but they remain important—sometimes even more important than our life's work itself. For example, the great musical composer Charles Ives couldn't make ends meet financially through his masterful compositions. So he worked in the insurance business in order to meet his basic needs while still devoting much time to writing the music for which he was poorly paid. Vincent van Gogh's paintings now bring millions on the auction market, but not so during his lifetime, when he was sustained by a caring brother. I know a gifted artist who similarly cannot earn an adequate living through her art, gifted though she is in different art forms. She earns her living through academic administration. She engages in that work with a caring, creative spirit even though that is not her main gift or purpose in life.

To be a mother or father is vocational in the deepest sense. We care for one another, we nurture young lives, we enjoy being together and doing things together. This requires considerable investments of time and energy.

There are other sub-vocations. There are many institutions and organizations that depend upon voluntary work for their successful operation. Parents of school-age children may invest time in the local PTA organization, knowing this impacts the quality of their children's educational experience. Most churches depend on laypeople for institutional service, including missional activities beyond the institution as well as caring for those in need.

The list of potential sub-vocations is endless, but I don't want to overlook vacation time. We need to take breaks, both physically and emotionally, but our choices of vacations can be relevant to our larger vocational commitments. Do they restore our relationships? Do they reconnect us with the wonders of the natural world? Do they include needed exercise?

There is one more vocational consideration: What happens when we are confronted, out of the blue, by an emergency that we are uniquely fitted to handle? Consider: You're driving along and suddenly come upon a car that has just run into a ditch. Other cars are continuing as though nothing has happened. Do you take the time to stop and render aid? That's the story line of Jesus's parable of the Good Samaritan in which a couple of respectable religious figures walked by an injured crime victim, ignoring him. Only someone from a hated religious group stopped to offer aid. There have been countless emergency situations—people getting caught in house fires, falling into deep water, being attacked by muggers or worse—where one could potentially save a life despite the personal risk. Isn't that a kind of calling? We didn't ask to be there, but there we are. The fact we are present means we must act if at all possible. It matters if we do.

Educational Implications

Most vocations require educational preparation whether in a collegiate setting or in a place of practical training. I do not question the relevance of practical education, but over the past few decades, I've noticed that job preparation has tended to crowd out other kinds of education. That seems to be true at both secondary and postsecondary levels.

Our society has largely lost track of the importance of a liberal arts education. Education does not exist simply to help us be better trained for the work force. It also exists to help us grow in maturity. This is relevant even to our place in the work force. Well-educated, thinking people can be more independent and productive.

It is certainly true that a well-educated person will likely do better in any of the professions that require creative and critical judgment. I suspect it may also be true of work in technological fields. In any case, we will certainly be more well-rounded people if we explore the broad range of cultural treasures available through education.

Vocational Integrity

In this chapter we have mostly considered vocational choices—choosing our life's work, devoting ourselves to sub-vocational activities, and treating emergency situations where our actions matter as a kind of vocational responsibility.

Now we will consider how we act within a chosen vocation when we are pushed to do things that violate our conscience. I once had a professor of ethics, also dean of my graduate school, who let it be known that he carried a letter of resignation in his pocket to be submitted if he were forced to act in a clearly unethical manner. Fortunately, for more than a quarter of a century, he never had to pull that letter out of his pocket. I don't think we need to follow that example, but we should all carry in the back of our minds a line we won't cross—even if it proves costly. Suppose you are engaged in medical research. The results of your studies, if reported accurately, may mean your firm will not win a lucrative new contract. Or, suppose you are working for a contractor who requires you to use shoddy, even dangerous, materials. Suppose you are a building inspector offered favors that amount to bribes to modify your report. Or, suppose you're a legislator being pushed by your party to vote for a bill that, in your best judgment, will go against the best interests of the people you serve. Suppose you are a preacher tempted to avoid unpopular topics even though you are convinced these are things the people need to hear.

The list can go on endlessly. No doubt we cannot always

be right, and no doubt there are sometimes compromises we have to make for the sake of a greater good. The late Senator William Fulbright was, in his time, a giant in helping to formulate wise US foreign policy, but his tenure was during the period when numbers of Southern political figures vowed to continue racial segregation. Fulbright, who knew better, did not challenge the racist laws and customs. Should he have drawn the line there? I think so, although by not doing so, he was able to continue his work on foreign policy. By contrast, Congressman Brooks Hays, also of Arkansas, refused to support the school segregation policies of Governor Orval Faubus. In the end, he lost the next election to a segregationist write-in candidate. Should Hays have compromised his beliefs to retain his seat? I do not think so. In the long run, his example inspired another generation of political figures with more progressive views. We cannot always accurately predict an outcome, but a critical part of our calling is to act with integrity.

Living out your vocation is a gift that brings enormous satisfaction in life. It is a matter worth pursuing seriously throughout your life.

A Note to Younger Readers

Here we have discussed the all-important question of our life's work. To speak of this as vocation is to remind ourselves that what we do is a calling. We can think of our work—and even what I've called sub-vocations—as a service of love to fellow humanity. For many Christians and adherents of other faiths, this is a response to the purposes of a loving God. Our sense of vocation about what we do can matter greatly.

CHAPTER 8

WHAT DOESN'T MATTER MUCH

Having taken up a number of things that matter greatly to us as individuals and participants in society, we turn now to things that don't matter all that much. These are things that are greatly emphasized in American culture and that focus the attention and efforts of large numbers of people. I wish to consider several of these, bearing in mind that each includes items that do matter, along with items that do not. I have in mind something like Aristotle's famous "golden mean." His idea was that we should find a middle ground "between excess and deficiency." The problem with the following three things is that American culture emphasizes them to excess.

1. Material Wealth Doesn't Matter Much

Let's start with wealth. Clearly, we do have material needs. We have to have enough resources to feed, clothe, and shelter ourselves as well as to meet the needs that depend on location and ordinary social requirements. If we are parents, we want to provide for our children. We have to be able to afford medical care, either projected or actual. Education costs money. Recreational needs are important and have to be met. Most of us also want to have a rainy-day fund for unforeseen expenses. The average individual or family budget often includes such things. I do not wish to downplay the fact that we all have need for some minimum level of income and savings.

When I refer to material wealth, I have something much more in mind. Some years ago, a college economics professor noted we do not have an unlimited need for any particular material item. We can get to the point where we have enough of almost anything we could name, but there is one thing, he said, for which our desire can be unlimited: money. Many of us feel we can never have enough.

We live in a materialistic age. We may not all want the same things, but we all want more money because it's required to buy the things we want. In a fascinating public television interview in June 2017, Warren Buffett talked about such things. Then listed as the fourth-richest person on earth (with wealth calculated then at about $75 billion), Buffett acknowledged that his principal objective through the years had been to acquire more and more wealth, largely through investments. He did not, however, seek wealth in order to buy more things. He could, he said, easily pay for ten more houses scattered around the country or for a five-hundred-foot yacht, but he had no need or desire for such things. He was perfectly content with his home in Omaha, which he had lived in for many years. While it is hardly a typical middle-class dwelling, it certainly is not a mega-mansion. Interestingly, he remarked that he thought he'd be happy enough living on $100,000 a year. While that figure is well above the median American income, it is still within the middle class. Buffett also reported he was happy in his work, remarking that at age 86 he still had a good deal of vigor and motivation.

My point is not to extol this multibillionaire, but to make the larger point that, despite his vast wealth, he had grasped this main point: money does not buy happiness. Of course money can buy things, but do things bring happiness? There may well be a momentary pleasure, but real life is about so much more than possessions. I don't know how to prove this, but I suspect a poor child receiving a much-desired birthday present may be just as happy, in purely psychological terms, as a billionaire with his next new yacht.

Jesus's familiar parable of the prosperous farmer makes a similar point. In his story, the farmer's crops were so abundant that he decided to build a much larger barn to store his grain, believing he had enough to last him many years. But he died that very night! Who then would receive all of his wealth?

Buddhism also teaches the folly of building our lives around possessions (or anything else in the physical world, for that matter). All things are ephemeral, destined to pass away. Nothing is permanent. Look around you. Do you see anything that will last forever? Certainly no plant or animal life. The longest-lasting things are, I suppose, the rocks. But even the earth itself is destined one day to be gone in one way or another. There is a folk song that says: "All things shall perish from under the sky. Music alone shall live…never to die." Maybe even music cannot last forever. We may think of our physical bodies as our primary possession, though it's obvious that no one's body is permanent.

How important it is to remember that, although we have to have some material things and a reasonably healthy body to survive, it is an illusion to build our lives around material possessions or to focus on them as if they were the meaning of our life.

During my college years I had to scramble just to make enough money to stay in school. At the end of my sopho-more year, I received a job offer that would have solved all of my problems. I could still be a student, no longer strapped for cash, but it would take a good deal of my time, and I'd have to live in a nearby town. What I would miss would be all the other enriching aspects of college and opportunities to develop leadership skills. I shared this opportunity with a wise counselor. After hearing me out, he said, "Phil, never make a decision on the basis of money unless you absolutely have to." I turned the job down, and it made all the difference in my having two more wonderful years of college experience. I even got by better financially than I thought possible. My mentor's advice was a greater gift than he could have known. Sometimes it is necessary to make a decision on the basis of money; often it is not.

In our materialistic society, we're bombarded with ways to gain wealth quickly. Many states now conduct lotteries, often with huge payouts for a very limited number of winners. We've all read stories of how the lives of big winners were practically ruined. We're also bombarded with opportunities to enjoy major savings on this or that purchase. Our culture pushes us to spend more and more. In the end, this is the meaningless pursuit of an illusion.

One final note: Sometimes people pursue wealth not for the happiness it could bring, but to have more than other people—a better house, a better car, a more expensive vacation, or some other symbolic expression of one's superiority over neighbors and other acquaintances. The idea or hope that better things will lead to more respect is also an illusion. Wealth is actually more likely to drive a wall between you and other people. We actually become less, not more, humanized. Conversely, there is no need to feel inferior if we have less material wealth than others.

2. Power Doesn't Matter Much

Not only does money not matter as much as we might believe, but power does not matter as much as we might think. We all need to possess some power both to achieve our vocational goals and to participate in the shaping of human history. But there can be an unhealthy desire for power. A tragedy of nondemocratic societies is that people are treated as things, with oppressive leaders monopolizing power for selfish ends. There are currently a number of oppressive regimes on several continents in which people are denied a meaningful share of power.

Seeking power in order to control the lives of others is self-destructive. Having treated other people as objects to be controlled, the powerful person has unwittingly reduced his or her own humanity to the power itself.

Some seek power for the adulation of multitudes. Think of a candidate for political office, facing thousands of cheering supporters. What an ego trip that must be! In many years of observing public figures in Washington, DC, I have concluded that people seek high office for one of two reasons: either they wish to *be* something greater than before, or they want to *do* something that will help others. I suppose there is often some mixture of these factors. Those who crave the adulation of multitudes may also want to serve them, and those whose primary motivation is service may rather enjoy the affirmation of large numbers of people as well. In extreme cases, a public figure may be so narcissistic that the common good is hardly any consideration at all. This is a tragedy both for the public figure and for those who are affected by the public figure's actions.

I suppose the acid test is the readiness of a public figure to do anything to stay in power or, on the other hand, to resign rather than seriously damage the public interest. As we have seen in chapter 4, a willingness to compromise remains important so long as it is for the sake of the public good. But that does not mean abandoning one's core convictions.

The point is that seeking power for its own sake and particularly to control others or to bolster a weak ego is an illusory, fleeting goal.

3. Fame Doesn't Matter Much

In good company with money and power is fame. We all need to be respected. Being famous is another matter. Celebrity status may be achieved through outstanding accomplishments. Great musicians, athletes, writers, or actors can be known and recognized by millions of people. Ordinary people often seek a share of that notoriety. I find it fascinating that people want to be seen on television, if only for a fleeting moment, not realizing that few will take any note.

There is a curious paradox common to celebrities. Fame is illusive. A best-selling novelist may feel unable to repeat the success. Celebrities in other fields may live in fear they will be found out as imposters, so they seek to prove to others or themselves that they have truly earned their successes.

There's another interesting dynamic about fame. A person may enjoy the public attention all the while forgetting that he or she is known principally for accomplishments in a very limited field. A great actor will be known for her movies but not for the wholeness of her personhood. A famous athlete will be known for prowess on the gridiron but not for any other aspect of his life. As such, the children of prominent parents may suffer greatly for their inherited fame. As young children, they may read about themselves in the media, not realizing that the media portrays them through a very limited lens. The relentless scrutiny of others is not without consequences and, often, psychological burdens.

So while fame may look enticing, it is both illusory and costly. The quest for fame for its own sake is not one to pursue.

A Note to Younger Readers

This may prove to be one of the most difficult chapters in the book, but in a book about what matters, we've had to contrast those points with what doesn't matter very much. Being richer than others, having more power than others, and possessing greater status than others are primary objectives of many people—particularly in a materialistic culture. Remember, though, these things are ephemeral, actually leading away from human fulfillment, not to it.

EPILOGUE

Your life matters and who you are matters, so I would be remiss to neglect one critical component to happiness. Cultivating a deep sense of gratitude is basic to human fulfillment. Without gratitude, we will never be fully satisfied or fully happy.

We can be grateful we are alive, not of our own choosing but through the choices of parents and long-forgotten ancestors. Each of them contributed to our emerging in a world teeming with life. We can be grateful for all the nurturing good that has brought us to where we are today.

We can be grateful for our capacity to discern truth and to reject falsehood—and to accept the truth that our own lives matter. We can be grateful for the gift of mind and the tug of curiosity, leading us on to new insights and challenges.

We can be grateful for our ability to become people of

119

integrity, to be centered upon the best that it is given to us to know, to grow in our capacity to love, to be kind, to be generous, to be patient, to be faithful to our commitments, and to know when to improve them.

We can be grateful for the gift of inherited religious traditions, pointing us toward the ultimate source of goodness, drawing us into fellowship with others with whom we share deeper values, and joining us in service to people in need and to the preservation and enhancement of the environment.

We can be grateful for the political order, offering us the opportunity to help shape history toward human good and resist evils and injustices.

We can be grateful for the gift of community, which ever enlarges our selfhood, embraces us in mutual caring, and draws us into a deeper grasp of our linkage to the entire family of humankind.

We can be grateful for educational opportunities beyond those available to many in previous generations and in some other parts of the world today, learning ever more about ourselves, our history, our traditions, and the social problems needing correction.

We can be grateful for opportunities to have vocational directions in life, blending our gifts with opportunities to serve others and having a deeper sense that our lives can serve purposes beyond our knowing.

We can even be grateful for our capacity to resist ephemeral goals of wealth, power, and status that divide us from others and detract from the nobility of true human possibilities.

Beyond the matters we have touched upon in this book, we can be grateful for the sheer beauty by which we are surrounded—the good green earth, the gentle life-sustaining rainfall, the lakes, the mountains, the song of the birds, the fishes of the streams and of the deep, and the treasures of art, science, and literature by which our lives have been lifted.

Most of all, I am grateful for the younger generation. You are so energetic, so gifted, so imaginative. You are the generation of the internet and social media. You are more inclusive in spirit, having largely rejected racism, homophobia, the lower status of women, and other divisive realities that have haunted human society for centuries. And you will write further chapters of human progress, in time, looking back upon lives of signal accomplishment as you pass the torch to yet further generations. I believe in you and have great hope for you as you go forth in gratitude, leaning in to the things that matter!

SPECIAL THANKS AND ACKNOWLEDGMENTS

I have not used academic footnotes in this writing, but the following acknowledgments may be useful to readers:

1. The references to Paul Tillich's definition of religion as "ultimate concern" in chapter 3 are from his *Systematic Theology Volume I* (Chicago: University of Chicago Press, 1951), especially 12–15.

2. The reference to H. Richard Niebuhr's concept of value center in chapter 3 is from his *Radical Monotheism and Western Culture* (New York: Harper and Row, 1960), especially the Introduction.

3. The James Carroll quote in chapter 3 is from his *Christ Actually* (London: William Collins, 2014), 42.

4. The column by Catherine Rampell, cited at the beginning of chapter 4, is from *The Washington Post*, August 16, 2016.

5. The Reinhold Niebuhr quote in chapter 4 is from Reinhold Niebuhr, *The Children of Light and the Children of Darkness: A Vindication of Democracy and a Critique of Its Traditional Defense* (Chicago: University of Chicago Press, 2011), xx.

6. The T. S. Eliot quotation at the beginning of chapter 5 is from his poem, "Choruses from the Rock," in his *The Complete Poems and Plays* (New York: Harcourt Brace Jovanovich, 1971), 103.

7. The words of Martin Luther, in chapter 7, are from his "Open Letter to the Christian Nobility of the German Nation Concerning the Reform of the Christian Estate," written in 1520.

8. The quotation from King James I of England, in chapter 7, is from his Speeches to Parliament, 1609. Cited in George H. Sabine, *A History of Political Theory* (New York: Henry Holt and Company, 1961), 396.

I am especially thankful to a number of people who read or heard parts of this book and offered suggestions. That includes a weekly lecture and discussion group I conduct in my Riderwood Village community. I especially appreciated thoughtful contributions by the late Audrey Beck, John Eliot, and Ron Ragland, although others were also helpful.

My wife, Carolyn, as always, has been supportive of this work and a perceptive interpreter of our grandchildren and their generation. I have dedicated this book to those grandchildren. Several of them offered valuable suggestions about what they would like to hear from my generation, and I have had them and the rest of the millennial generation principally in mind as I've written this book.

And I am grateful for the perceptive work of Abingdon editors Susan Salley, Dawn Woods, Jennifer Day, and Susan Cornell. They confirm my belief that good editors are a writer's best friends!